Theodore F Price

Heroes of the Spanish-American War

Theodore F Price

Heroes of the Spanish-American War

ISBN/EAN: 9783744714235

Printed in Europe, USA, Canada, Australia, Japan

Cover: Foto ©ninafisch / pixelio.de

More available books at **www.hansebooks.com**

HEROES

OF THE

SPANISH-AMERICAN WAR

AND

Lyre and Sword of Spain:

TWO EPIC POEMS

BY

THEODORE F. PRICE

Author of "Heroes of Santiago," "Ballads of the Western Wilds," "Epic of the Poets," etc.

NEW YORK:
1899.

TO

Admiral George Dewey, U. S. N.,

WHO HAS EXALTED HIS COUNTRY'S STANDARD HIGH AMONG NATIONS; TO HIS WORTH AS A REPRESENTATIVE AMERICAN; TO HIS GENIUS AS STATESMAN AND DIPLOMAT, AND GALLANTRY AS AN OFFICER, THIS WORK IS RESPECTFULLY DEDICATED BY

THE AUTHOR.

Contents.

	Page.
PRELUDE	9

PART I.
WHERE RODE THE MAINE	21
THE DEMONS' MINE	31

PART II.
MCKINLEY	39
LEADERS OF MEN	49
NAVAL CHIEFS	61

PART III.
DEWEY	69
THE ASIAN SQUADRON	79
THE CRUISERS' CAPTAINS	89

PART IV.
WAR'S LEVIATHANS	97
THE EVE OF BATTLE	103
PASSING THE BOCA GRANDÉ	109
MANILA	119

PART V.
THROUGH HOSTILE WATERS	137
BATTLE OF MANILA BAY	143
VICTORY AT CAVITÉ	155

PART VI.
THE SURRENDER	165
AFTER THE BATTLE	173

ROMANCE OF THE ARAB CONQUEST	183
LOVE AND WAR IN MOORISH GRENADA	187
SPAIN'S HERO POETS	197
DECLINE OF SPAIN'S GOLDEN AGE	207

Illustrations.

	Page.
PRESIDENT WM. MCKINLEY	Frontispiece.
ON THE BEACH AT CAPE MAY	19
CAPT. CHAS. D. SIGSBEE, late of cruiser Maine . .	31
LIEUT.-COMMANDER RICHARD WAINWRIGHT . . .	39
JUDGE WM. R. DAY, of Ohio, late Secretary of State, etc.	49
HON. JOHN D. LONG, Secretary of Navy . . .	61
HON. THEODORE ROOSEVELT, Governor N. Y. . .	64
ADMIRAL GEORGE DEWEY, U. S. N.	69
THE OLYMPIA, Admiral Dewey's Flag-ship . . .	79
CAPT. JOSEPH B. COGHLAN, of cruiser Raleigh, U. S. N.	89
COL. JOHN HAY, Secretary of State . . .	97
HON. LYMAN J. GAGE, Secretary of Treasury . .	103
HON. JOHN W. GRIGGS, N. J., Attorney-General . .	109
PHILIPPINO LADY, Spanish-Mestizo	119
LIEUT. THOMAS B. BRUMBY, Dewey's Flag-officer .	137
BATTLE OF MANILA BAY	143
HON. RUSSELL A. ALGER, Secretary of War . .	155
BRIG.-GEN'L HENRY C. CORBIN, Adjutant-General .	165
HON. CHARLES EMORY SMITH, Postmaster-General	173
MAJ.-GEN'L FITZHUGH LEE	179

Prelude.

I.

WITH longings for the breakers' roar,
    Wild Nature's scenes, I ceased to roam.
  Found waiting me this sea-girt home,
Charmed with the near-by breakers' roar!

II.

Where shines in play bright silver spray,
    Fringing the swells that evermore
    Each other follow o'er and o'er,
Whose ceaseless roll time may not stay:

III.

At morn, when day's orb disappears
    And Dian rides upon the wave,
    And when the seething billows rave,
The sea sounds ever in my ears;

IV.

Tall, white-wing'd ships move slowly on,
   That seem as sailing on the land,
   Where blue waves blend with shining sand,
And sea and sky seem merged in one:

V.

Huge dolphins leap, and plunging, wheel,
   In sport would dare the gulls in air:
   Their black flukes rear o'er waters clear
Whose glittering sides near storms reveal.

VI.

The sun-rise gilds green meadow lands,
   South spreads Old Ocean's waters blue;
   South-west, where naught obstructs the view,
The light-house picturesquely stands.

VII.

When Nature's forces fierce engage
   In thund'rous strife, 'mid gloom profound,
   Loud Ocean roars! Flash lightnings round!
Sublime this elemental rage!

VIII.

Mov'd by the grandeur of the storm,
   There is that in its voice sublime
   Bears one beyond the things of time,
Wild Nature's wondrous, startling charm!

IX.

The din of war by land and sea,
   Blent with the roar of surges, came
   And seemed to sound each hero's name,
Commingling with the bathers' glee!

X.

A dream-land voice, 'mid war's alarms,
   Bade me track battles' heroes on,—
   In visions,— 'neath the tropic sun,
There celebrate their deeds of arms!

XI.

A woven woof of diverse hues
   The spirit pictures of the time,
   'Mid strife at sea, 'mid scenes sublime,
Where tropic shores rich shades diffuse:

XII.

Portray'd that deed of demons dark,
  Spain's challenge for her fatal war,
  Where that wreck'd cruiser's ruins are,
Where mines did fiendish murderers' work!

XIII.

Thoughts still through scenes ensanguined rove,
  Far o'er the wave clear vision soars
  Beyond Pacific's startled shores,
Where DEWEY's dauntless cruisers move!

XIV.

Before me, o'er the Gulf's expanse,
  Armed squadrons, transports, convoys passed
  With CAPTAIN TAYLOR's cruiser vast,
Staunch Indiana, in advance!

XV.

Where SAMPSON's watchful squadron rides
  Brave HOBSON sinks the Merrimac,
  Across CERVERA's outward track,
In Santiago's winding tides!

XVI.

The white-wing'd ships that pass me by
  Bring visions of contending fleets!—
  CERVERA swift destruction meets
Beneath the iron hail of SCHLEY!

XVII.

With heroes ROOSEVELT and WOOD
  I charge victorious! dauntless still,
  While hidden foes their comrades kill,
Till the foe flee o'er trails of blood!

XVIII.

Commingling with those gallant men,
  The Riders Rough of ROOSEVELT,
  I hear the Mauser bullets pelt
'Mid Guasima's bloody glen:

XIX.

I seek in vain the Spanish wolf,—
  Gazing with shaded brow afar,—
  Whose cruisers sunk, shot-riddled are
Where Cuba meets the Mexic Gulf!

XX.

While stirring sounds still come to me,
    While strife by land and sea appalls,
    To SHAFTER Santiago falls,
Whose heroes made the lorn isle free!

XXI.

Ere long Commissioners of Peace,
    From Paris, tell that this brief war
    Confers fair isles, some near, some far,
Which Spain to this land must release!

XXII.

The Cape's brave pilots tell a tale
    Of ship and gallant Captain lost,
    When breakers lash the storm-swept coast,
Where rages oft the wrathful gale!

XXIII.

The skipper of that fated ship,
    Whom scarce two decades had pass'd o'er,
    In manhood's vigor left the shore,
To make from the Bay's mouth his trip;

XXIV.

Kiss'd his young wife and babe, his pride,
   Smil'd o'er its mother's fond concern,
   Bespoke safe voyage, quick return,
And with his staunch crew stemm'd the tide:

XXV.

Off Cape Henlopen's misty light,
   'Mid February's blinding snows,
   While o'er the shrouds wild billows froze,
Fierce raged the winds that wintry night!

XXVI.

The Storm-King blew a mighty blast!
   The schooner on her beam ends bowl'd
   Then, in the sea's trough helpless roll'd,
Before the tempest driving fast!

XXVII.

'Twixt sea and sky, on breakers hung,
   Masts creaking 'neath each close-reef'd sail,
   Despair turn'd crew and Captain pale
When with warp'd seams a-leak she sprung!

XXVIII.

Before the gallant craft went down,
    Each man, exhausted, seized his oar,
    Pulled thro' huge breakers, reach'd the shore,
And strayed, dazed, freezing toward the town:

XXIX.

Joy filled each breast to reach the land,
    For life e'en thankful, saved from wreck.
    Though stripp'd of all, time brings all back,
With waiting loved ones near at hand:

XXX.

The Captain soon was left alone,
    Lost in the driving, blinding snow,
    Wand'ring confused, benumbed and slow,
Whose crew by obscured paths had gone!

XXXI.

Escaped in vain the Ocean's wrath,
    Raged the land demon's midnight gale!
    'Mid blinding blasts his footsteps fail,
From comrades strayed beyond the path:

XXXII.

Toiling 'mid darkness, snow and frost,
   Grown weaker through each weary hour,
   Each frozen nerve bereft of power,
He sank at last, in death's sleep,—lost!

XXXIII.

'T was morn, 't was eve, day went and came;
   The young wife waited, wept in vain,
   Their child caressed, and bore her pain,
While sea-winds seemed to breathe his name:

XXXIV.

Some days had passed; a friend at last,
   Amid a wood the town beyond,
   Beside a tree the Captain found,—
There frozen,—sitting as at rest!

XXXV.

The pilot tells the tale to-day:
   The daughter fair and graceful grew,
   Became a wife, fond mother, too,
Where sounds the surge, where dolphins play.

XXXVI.

Obedient has the poet been,—
   I sang of war by land and sea,
   As pictured visions came to me,
As I, perchance, shall sing again:

XXXVII.

Now, in the soft September haze,
   The poet must his harp resign:
   For changeful destiny is mine,
And duty ends the dreamy days.

Cape May, N. J.,
   Sept. 30, 1898.

ON THE BEACH AT CAPE MAY.

Heroes of the Spanish American War.

Heroes of the Spanish-American War.

PART FIRST.

Where Rode the Maine.

I.

WHERE yon proud stronghold's spires appear,
Whose gloomy Morro guards her bay,
Their doom is life-long, prison'd there,
'Neath dark oppression's jealous sway:
The stranger at that city's gate
Suspicion sends to RUIS' fate;
And here CISNEROS, patriot maid,
Escapes a prison's living tomb,
Whose beauty, worth, gains generous aid,
Wins love, fond friends in Freedom's home,

Americanos languish, long
In noisome dungeons know despair,
Enduring hate's most heinous wrong,
For name alone must horrors share:
For, Spain would guess these shall redress,
Avenge, ere long, the isle's distress!

For those who strive just rights to gain,
Who rashly loud of wrongs complain,
Wait Morro's walls and cankering chain!

Gaul's Bastile dread might scarce disclose,—
Ere crushed 'neath retribution's blow,—
More fearful sum of human woes
Than this grim castle's annals show:
May ruin as complete befall
Her dungeon by Havana's wall!

II.

Pearl of the isles in Mexic wave!
Land of the mango, orange, palm,
Of coral grots warm waters lave,
Loud storms sublime and seasons calm;

Fair flowers that cheer, whose perfumes please,
Mottling the vistas bright between;
Dense thickets, quivering in the breeze,
Broken by brake and deep ravine,—
Of darkest tragedies the scene,—
'T was meet that here his dust might rest
Whose firm foot first the New World prest:

Here Santiago still remains
Most ancient city on this strand;
His capital built, whence, in chains,
He sail'd back to that thankless land,—
Though not the country of his birth,—
Enrich'd by him o'er all on earth:

III.

Since Genoa's discov'rer moored
His caravals in Cuba's bay,
Four centuries her race endured
The cruel Spaniard's blighting sway;
Where tropic vales of fadeless green
Bloom through the ever-circling year;

Spring, Autumn, hand in hand, are seen,
Majestic palms, rich slopes appear,—
Cool, shadowy groves with waters clear,
Pineapples sweet warm breezes shake,
The plant of fragrant fume grows; where
Berry that cheers, the sugary brake,—
Where human hearts ne'er cease to ache!

Here, Native homes all joys forsake,
Whose race strives Nature's charms among;
Whose all, whose life the ruthless take,
Crush'd 'neath all forms of cruel wrong!

IV.

Those peoples bleed at every vein
Where barb'rous Spain would rule maintain!
Whose crimes this age humane disgrace
That stain'd her past:
      LEE, to her face,
Lorn Cuba's ghastly horrors bared,—
Whole provinces in dying throes!—
Boldly the hideous truth declared,

Nor failed their slayer to disclose,
While fiends their sea-sunk mine prepared—
Vengeful assassins!—darkly dared
That savage deed!
                Time's scroll shall place
'Mong Spain's dread deeds of many an age,—
Burnt in her blood-bedabbled page,—
This crime, that crowns unreasoning rage,
That sounds her final doom's presage!

* * * * * * *
* * * * * * *

V.

By frowning Morro's bastions dun
Rode grandly the majestic Maine,
While slowly sank Havana's sun,
Dying the waves a crimson stain:
Prophetic hue!—Alas, how few
Of all her unsuspecting crew
Shall fond ones press, greet friends again!

  Sigsbee looks from his vessel's side,
That Captain of inventive mind

Who sounded seas of deepest tide
With device planned great depths to find,
Fruit of his thought:
                      With practiced eye
His cruiser staunch he views with pride,—
While polished guns, bright brass ablaze,
Gleam in the sun's expiring rays,—
Nor dreams dread doom is pending nigh,
O'er many brave men here to die
E're dawn shall gild the mourning sky!

  While treachery's oft-recurring signs
Teach thought to seek suspicion's lines,
The Captain unseen ill divines,
Cool, cautious, prudent:
                      What avail,
While duty calls where fiends prevail!
This deck is doom'd! Fate's thund'rous call
Bids him command the arm'd St. Paul!
Whose guns avenging, off San Juan,
Shall bear Spain's threatening Terror down!

VI.

Does WAINWRIGHT dream of death and
    wreck?—
The Officer Executive,—
CERVERA's dash, the Gloucester's deck?
That Porto Rico fame shall give?
That he shall be the last to leave
As this rent hulk sinks 'neath the wave?

  Schooling the brave Lieutenant gained
That makes him seaman to the core;
Though lean in figure, athlete trained:
Six feet in stature,—trifle more;
Firm muscles, sinews, o'er which reign
Cool judgment, broad, well-balanced brain,—
With keen blue eyes whose light is born
From merriment, or lit by scorn:
Yet middle manhood to attain,
E'en now wears marked impressive mien:

  Bold WAINWRIGHT's stirring future pierce!
Look, while his guns diminutive

The enemy's "destroyers" fierce,—
Pluton and Furor,—death-blows give,
To blaze on Santiago's shore!
As though by suicidal hand,
To burst the wreck-strewn waters o'er!
Whose hulks long mark the vanquished strand:

'Mid that momentous battle's roar,
Attacked each Spanish craft in sight,
In hottest fire of that fierce fight,
Gloucester's Commander clears his score!

VIII.

As evening's length'ning shadows sped,
While WAINWRIGHT paused by SIGSBEE's side,
Answering salute, the Captain said,
Impressed with sense of danger nigh:
"Our men may have their courage tried
Ere we to Morro bid good-bye!"
To which his aide made light reply,
Casting a glance at wave and sky,
And both, the cabin's precincts hide:

The restless crew strolled to and fro,
Held where fresh evening breezes blew,
To watch each wave's slow-swelling flow,—
Dyed violet or deeper blue,—
Breathing the balmy evening dew:
On deck the few conversed this hour,
The tropic clime's soft influence knew,
While sea-birds swooped to warn, where lower
The bolts of doom, the dread mine's power!

IX.

'Mong these there be oft musing still,
Through youth's fond scenes, would joys retrace
The home, the hill, the trysting place;
The fair, the sweetly-smiling face,
Affection's pledge! The spirit yearns
To clasp her form in fond embrace,
While faithful memory returns,
And for loved friends the bosom burns:

Some seek repose, no morn to know,
Hurl'd from sweet sleep, when cares seemed fled,

By bolts volcanic hid below,
By demons sprung from horror's bed!
Atrops but waits to cut the thread
That holds their ship o'er Ocean's grave,
To close o'er those, life's morn scarce fled,
Whom human arm shall fail to save,
Strewn mangled o'er Havana's wave!

CAPT. CHARLES D. SIGSBEE,
LATE OF THE CRUISER MAINE.

The Demons' Mine.

I.

MISSION'D to save her dying race,
    LEE went lorn Cuba's scenes among,
Saw woe's increase, oppression base,—
Portrayed the isle's appalling wrong,
The deadly blight of ages long:

Far more than this the Consul saw:
That justice was not of the law
By which his countrymen were tried;
And, with his Nation thus defied,
A dark menace hung o'er the tide!

In peace the Maine would here abide,
Offence unsought 'gainst Spanish pride:
E'en after horror's pending day,

When, welcomed, in Manhattan's Bay
Viscaya unmolested lay.

Let craft, base subterfuge maintain
Her evil fame, her treacherous name,
Swift ruin waits just war's proclaim,—
The tyrant's loss, the freeman's gain!

* * * * * * *
* * * * * * *

II.

The lone watch treads the silent deck,
The lookout high scans each far speck,
While gone below, the gallant crew
Ambitions view of many a hue,
Or, wrapped in peaceful, dearer dreams
Of home and friends, afar from war,
With sweethearts stray by brightest streams,
By northern lakes, by prairies far:

Sits Captain Sigsbee, undisturbed,
Where cabin walls their calm confer,
Unwarned of dread doom's near alarm,

THE DEMONS' MINE. 33

O'er day's last duties deep absorbed,
Ere ANTHONY, with ceremonious air,—
'Mid mad destruction's fiery storm,—
To tell of ruin, shall appear!

III.

Night's shades sank darker o'er the deep,
Pierc'd by lights twinkling on the wave;
The good ship, like her crew, asleep,
The drowsy tides caressing lave:

Soft winds blow from some spring-kist shore,
Balmy and sweet as breath of May,
Cooled by the icebergs drifting o'er,
Where snows of February lay —
That down to southern regions stray—
Till Sol in Cancer rules the day,
And warms the Greenland seas; whose gale
Cools the Gulf-stream, whose broad, deep way
Pours through Atlantic's wave its trail,
And toward Spain's shores bears many a sail

* * * * * * *
* * * * * * *

IV.

HARK,—that far-rolling, thund'rous boom!
That rends the evening's still profound,
Rumbling the deep, like earthquake's sound!—
Appalling as the crack of doom,—
Shaking ships, Morro's shores around!

Colossal cascades rend the gloom,
Like Hecla's geysers, mounting high,—
Blent fire and smoke, wild wave and sky!

Where the Maine mark'd the bay's expanse
Huge pillars blaze with glare intense!
Flames, mingling high their crimson dye,
Shot through black-rolling vapors dense!

A hail of steel,—war's giant arms!—
A shower of limbs, crush'd, mangl'd forms!—
All in tumultuous ruin roll'd!—
All in the demon's fiery fold!

Near vessels sound sharp, quick alarms!
Whose life-boats swiftly cleave the wave,
The maimed and dying men to save,

THE DEMONS' MINE.

Hurl'd far the wreck-strewn waters o'er!
Though of that brave crew many a score
Shall man the thund'ring guns no more:

V.

  The patriots died,—unhear'd their groan,—
Their marr'd forms o'er dark waters strewn
Where gloomy tides mourn as they flow,
Where somber sea-fowl make reply;
Where vultures fly expectant nigh;
Wolves of the waves, sharks lurk below:

  Sons, husbands, brothers, lovers slain,
Who died for Freedom,—not in vain!—
The watch-word lives o'er sea and plain:
Remember they who manned the Maine!

  Where battle's ship rode fair and strong,
Her waist with tripple steel enwound,
A smoking hulk, half-sunk among
The tangled wreckage strewn around,—
Down sinking deeper in the slime,—
Remains of all that work sublime!

While of his honor boasting loud,
That death-trap, sprung by Spaniard's hand,
Had hurl'd to death that hapless band,—
One common grave, one watery shroud!

VI.

Appall'd, enraged,—but not dismay'd,
By this dread stroke alarmed, awoke,
The Nation swift her ranks arrayed:
Her bugles gave the call: "To arms!"
And filled the land with loud alarms!

War's stirring mandates rouse the brave
From Canada to Mexic wave!
From Maine to California's strand,
From shores washed by clear Northern lakes,
Each city, village through the land
The spirit of the hour partakes!

Columbia's defenders swarm
On foot, by train, o'er hill and plain,—
From shop, school, bourse, bank, office, farm,
Men rally to avenge the Maine!

Like magic, thronging camps appear
With myriad thousands far and near!
To break oppression's power they come,—
The hope and flower of Freedom's home:

They come, they go,—nor long may wait,—
From San Francisco's Golden Gate,
For Asian isles, for Indies bound;
For Chickamauga's crimson ground.
On, to the shores of Florida,
To Jacksonville and Tampa Bay!

Augmenting still the legions fill,
Impatient of each brief delay;
In battle's evolutions drill
Till fleets convey the ranks away
To where red fields of carnage lay!

VII.

Thick-gathering war-clouds roll on high:
Signs of redress, of vengeance loom,—
Gloom redly 'gainst the northern sky
Whereon the Spaniard reads his doom!

THE DEMONS' MINE.

While retribution's stroke delayed,
The bigot nation,—self-betrayed,—
By pride besotted, cruel, crazed,
Against herself her rash hand raised,
Nor sure destruction might evade:

Insidious Spain! Your vampire brood,—
Of blacken'd heart and jaundic'd brain,—
Shall not on Cuba's throat retain
Remorseless clutch, athirst for blood!

Rose high, full-orb'd, the Queen of Night
And bathed her tresses in the main;
O'er heaven's dome shed effulgence bright,
In pale light veiled her starry train;
A group, her retinue, remain
To serve their mistress; Everywhere
She rules o'er her far-spread domain,—
Whose mirrors are all waters clear,—
Smiles on the dead who know not care,
The young, the valliant, the brave,
Who died where rolls Havana's wave.

LIEUT.-COMMANDER RICHARD WAINWRIGHT, U. S. N.

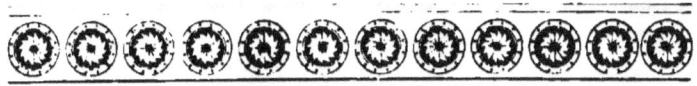

Heroes of the Spanish-American War.

PART SECOND.

McKinley.

I.

THERE is a peace that enervates,
  That weakens more than strengthens states,—
Yet, well might leader hesitate
To ope' the gates to strife's red tide,
Whose surge rolls thund'ring far and wide!
The country's councils may divide,—
Her unpreparedness well concealed,—
While well the statesman knows to wait
Ere sending men to war's red field.

McKINLEY.

No President ere found a time
For purpose higher, more sublime;
Faced problems more perplexing, stern;
Met issues of more vast concern,
Than greets now the Chief Magistrate
So honored by his people great;
Who dignifies, adorns the place
His countrymen called him to grace;

   And while he wears far-reaching cares
The peoples' good guides everything
That on his mind that pressure bears,
Which war's tremendous issues bring:

   The Nation's Chief at times must stand
Alone, opposed on every hand,
'Gainst all, imbued with sense of right,
Crushing disaster by his might:

   Yielding, he would have ruined all,—
For, blame on him alone must fall!
Decision formed, he stands his ground
Nor fails to prove his logic sound;

The Nation has a thinking mind,
Giving to thought's convictions vent:
No censors' rules expression bind,—
Adjusting ills thus brings content
Thereby explosions to prevent
As burst from forces closely pent!

II.

Each class shall reason as it may:
Finance, law, trade, schools have their say:
Clerk, club-man, craftsman seeks some flaw;
The exquisite, the gilded youth,
The chronically dissatisfied,—
With idiosyncrasies uncouth,—
Must either praise or strictures draw!
Wise Solons must their mandates give
To guide the Chief Executive;
Who, with all wisdom thus supplied,
Must still be more than Argus-eyed!

Without that knowledge intimate
Of statecraft's complicated things,—

Of issues that thereto relate,—
That long association brings,
'Tis not the wisest thing, always,
To critically blame or praise:
Who in such vaporings logic find
That typifies the reasoning mind?

While those there be who make complain,
Enlightened millions well sustain;
And those most competently wise
Most hesitate to criticise!

III.

The land's constructive energy
Its varied needs has more than filled:
Overproduction's vast supply
Each industries' demand has still'd:
Works of all crafts unpurchased rest;
O'erstocked the North, South, East and West,
As myriads unemployed attest;
While 'neath stagnation's gloomy shroud
Trade for new outlets clamors loud!

Good men, as hungry suppliants, ask
In vain employment day by day,
Rejoiced to find whatever task,—
Toiling for less than slender pay,—
While life's cares multiplying come,
With grim Want menace love and home!

V.

The army now provides a way,
Whose ranks absorb the unemployed,
The idle myriads!
    These be they,
Hope, home, ambition, peace destroyed,
Eating their hearts out day by day,
Who, unlodged, foot-sore tramp the way;

These help to swell the conquering ranks,
Ere long to win the Nation's thanks;
And these, though thronging ills await,
In logic's eyes, are fortunate!
Whose arms demands for wares have made,
Unlocking rich isles' ports of trade;

Wide opening every market's gate
While the world lauds their victories great!

* * * * · * * *

VI.

   Strife's spirit slept: gone factious years
Of blood and tears, of griefs and fears,
When North and South drew hostile blade,
In battle's panoply arrayed;
When sullen Spain,—long ill-concealed,—
Her dark assassin's hand revealed!
Standing with reeking dagger drawn,
While retribution's waves roll on;
Ere long to reach and deep o'erwhelm
Her plundered, her distracted realm!

   The olive brow grows dark with hate:
"War!" the deluded Don declares!—
"The Yankee Pigs!" and "Will they fight?"
Are terms assailing Woodford's ears:
Whose passports bid his mission cease,
While Madrid makes an end of peace!

Doubt clouds not now the statesman's brow,
Before the Chief his way lies clear;
Though tasks colossal face him, how
Prompt when emergencies appear!
The vigorous mind, strong hand are here;
The reasoner trained to thought profound,
Of quick perception, judgment sound.

VII.

Time heals all wounds, strong balm applies,
One common cause now unifies:
Now Blue and Gray join hand-in-hand
Where horror blights a neighboring strand
Enlightened laws to give the land;
Sustain the Nation's widening fame
'Neath one flag of unblemished name!

Should retribution longer wait,
While mourns the land o'er Cuba's fate,
Her isle of beauty desolate?
The statesman's words, the people's songs,
Their constant theme is Cuba's wrongs!

Shall not this blight that plagues the earth,
So near the home of Freedom's birth,
From this fair realm be driven forth?

In this humanitarian day
Shall not Columbia's potent ray
O'er the Gulf's isles benignant play?

 *   *   *   *   *   *   *
 *   *   *   *   *   *   *

VIII.

His well-knit form bends not to care,
Who must to supreme problems rise;
A native dignity is there
Beneath consummate mental poise:
In daily walk, in Senate Hall,
His greeting kind extends to all:

Not to be swayed from sense of right,
He consults still the people's will,
Whose every act fears not the light,
Whose mind progressive motives fill;
With sterling traits the world calls great,

Whose youth was trained to arts of war,
Made of such stuff as patriots are:

His fostering care, with well-won peace,
Sends life through all the ranks of trade:
As Sol's rays ice-locked streams release,
Long in dark Winter's garb arrayed:
Like sun-burst in bright morn of spring
That vivifies, warms everything!

At whose call rose that mighty host,—
And when peace dawned, so proudly penned
His Message, saying, not in boast:
"No prisoner fell to foeman's hand,
No gun in war, no vessel lost!"
Such is the land's Chief Magistrate,
Who serves his country well and state:
May honor guard the soul well tried,
And highest inspirations guide!

JUDGE WILLIAM R. DAY, OF OHIO.
LATE SECRETARY OF STATE AND PRESIDENT OF THE PARIS
PEACE COMMISSION.

Leaders of Men.

I.

THE President tried men and strong
   Made councilors in great affairs
When war raged sea and shore along,—
Departments' heads with heavy cares;
Chose aides whose keen acumen then
Met greatest nations' shrewdest men;
Designs most complicate to scan,
While the land shook to deepest core,
From where the Gulf's warm surges roar
To the far isles off Asia's shore!

II.

DAY's sterling worth past years had shown,
Betwixt whom and his Chief had grown

Warm friendship which time firmer made,—
Ever by word and deed displayed,—
Nor knows decay while locks grow gray,
While each pursues fame's upward way:

At duty's clarion call he came,
The Nation's mandates to obey,
Where honors high adorn his name,-
Urged not by thought of gain or fame.

DAY's was the hand, the guiding mind,—
By DAVIS, GRAY, FRYE. REID sustained,—
That statesmen's group, which lines defined,
Which Paris saw, for peace convened;
Spain's forfeit island realms that gave,
Through which was valor's guerdon gained,
Won by the land's defenders brave:

Puissant mind! Naught warps astray
From just decision! Governor's chair
Should be Ohio's gift! With clear
Untarnished name, such record fair,
Place the Peace Arbitrator there!

Whose acumen might well command,
Whose towering genius should command
Highest tribunal in the land!

III.

Diplomat, poet, statesman HAY,—
Whose youth was trained 'mid battle's stir,
Whom the Emancipator's care,
His erudite biographer,
Well launched on honor's high career,—
From Britain's court, with wreaths of bay,
Comes to the Secretary's chair;
Grasps the portfolio of State,
Equipp'd to well negotiate,
With men most eminent, the great:

No bigot this broad-minded man,
Who grasps the most far-reaching plan
With deepest penetration's ken,
Well-match'd 'gainst nations' shrewdest men.

* * * * * * *
* * * * * * *

IV.

War's Secretary now must wrest
With problems stern on every hand;
From north and south, from east and west,
Vast armies muster, train each band,
Convey munitions, build, invent,
Rear strong defences on each strand;
For gathering thousands must provide,
With methods new, with men untried,
Where much must be experiment;
Too much to hands untried must leave
To mischievous complications weave
Ere system can from chaos rise!

On ALGER most stupendous task
War's hasty preparation threw;
Who must a plotting foe unmask,
Aides competent unfound, or few,—
O'er war's arts peace had mantle thrown,—
While fields of carnage valor won
Became again contention's bone
Where critics raged with boldest tone!

V.

War, those to high positions drew
To lord o'er men outspoken, frank;
Knaves, o'er their betters placed by rank,
To whom dictation's post was new;
Who, garb'd in military cut,
Chance o'er stern men placed in command,
Offending by assumption's strut
Those who to lead were better plann'd;
Authority at whose expense
These show with lack of tactful sense!
Such petty despots, so 'tis said,
When 'gainst the foe are forces led,—
In action ranks grown less defined,—
Fall, on occasion, 'mong the dead,
Slain by chance missile from behind!

VI.

The army has evolved a mind,—
Old forms are dead, new thoughts prevail!
Crude discipline no more may bind,
Where mediæval despots fail;

Whose modes debasing must away,—
Knout, thumb-cord, stocks have had their day!

Science has come to lend her aid,
O'er battle's plain proclaims her sway,
Where progress mighty change has made
As chiefs of war can not gainsay!

Columbia's soldier has a soul
Where reason reigns! In man, not thing,
Injustice leaves its burning sting!
Enlighten'd ranks commands obey
From men who bid high manhood rule!

VII.

Seeing the blue line winding high
Up San Juan hill to win or die,
Unwavering till Spain's minions fly!
Britain's attaché fain would say,
Taking the field-glass from his eye:
"'T is greater than Balaclava!"

Spirit initiative gives,

Those whose fair fame on Time's scroll lives!
Whose conquering ranks, untried, undrill'd,
A world's unbounded praise compell'd!
Men's plaudits won, in tactics skill'd,
Train'd minds from many an Old World field!
Unfalt'ring still they bravely fought,—
Heroic band!
       Unstay'd by aught,
The gallant ranks press on and bleed,
Nor skulking minion stay to heed,
Enthus'd the enemy to meet,
Finding the way to save defeat,
Whose valor never knows retreat!

  Their arms resistless what shall stay!
Though foes outnumber, fierce the fray,
Seen, or where conceal'd foemen lay,
Charging where murd'rous Mausers slay,
Their line winds 'round El Caney's top,
Bearing the flag, in firm array,
Through blazing trenches, on and up,
Till Spaniards flee, when won the day!

VIII.

What ill conditions must they face,
From peaceful paths call'd forth to wage
Unequal strife, compell'd to race
'Gainst fevers, dread miasmas rage!

Much Freedom of her sons demands,—
Soldiers, she bids them still be men!
While far their widening realm expands,
Compelling law's enlighten'd reign
O'er many an isle, o'er fruitful strand,
With purpose high, with mission grand!

With SHAFTER's methods who, indeed,
Such marvelous record e'er had made!
Prompt action, victory shall excuse
Manœuvers some would fain abuse:
Let such confess,—whose words assail'd
Movements that valor made succeed,—
Others to do as much had fail'd!
Let none forget successful plan
Must be adapted to the man!

IX.

What potent Chief from war may free
Those evils manifold that be
On every field?
                Who shall invent
Such dread device to all 'twere death
Inevitable e'en to scent
Annihilation's fatal breath?

  Horrors of battlefields appall,
For, ever dear is human life;
Then, grown accustom'd to the strife,
The sounds of carnage lighter fall!
When first of crimson fields we hear,
What gallant souls so bravely bear,
Woes rend the breast, groans wound the ear;
Ere long, the milder grief finds vent,
Grown used to war's concomitant.

  What marvel, when brave armies bled,—
Although this land with plenty ran,—
The lines, at times, scant rations fed
Ere could be shaped more proper plan,

Those myriad details be supplied,
With men and measures all untried,
Unraveling many a tangled skein
Where untold complications reign;
What mind might sense plagues should prevail
Where ills unlook'd-for camps assail!

X.

The Adjutant industrious well
His o'erwrought Chieftain's hands sustain'd:
To CORBIN onorous duties fell,
Myriad colossal wants to meet,—
Department's o'ergrown needs maintain'd
Through crude formation's varying state,—
Whose tasks by day nor night abate,
While credit oft from merit shorn,
Fills honor's chair with many a thorn!

XI.

Sinues of gold! Let GAGE provide
The treasure vast on war's demand,
From the land's wealth to be supplied!

Squadrons and armies must expand,
Must be sustain'd, on sea and field,
From funds exhaustless coffers yield!

With elements the Treas'rer deals,
Which, jarred by an unsteady hand,
Spread wide disaster through the land,
Whose slightest shock the Nation feels!

XII.

That grand old State of sea-girt shores,
Her statesman sage and genial son,
GRIGGS, makes reflected honors hers!
New Jersey favor high confers
On him who Governor's laurels won,
Whose greatness 'neath her eye has grown!

Whose patriot heart and legal mind
Declares, in no uncertain tone,
Those isles his country's hand is on,—
O'er which protection's folds are thrown,
Which despot hand shall ne'er bring down,—
Magellan's realm must victory crown!

XIII.

The patriot heart warms to the name
CHARLES EMORY SMITH, unfailing friend
Of men who for their country stand:
Chief guardian of the Nation's mails,
Who to far-reaching duties came
With intricate conditions fraught;
Whose probity no man assails,
Practical earnest man of thought,
Who loves the right, wrong deeply feels;
Whose logic sound with force appeals
Through diction clear; whose eloquence
Brings firm conviction to the sense!

HON. JOHN D. LONG,
SECRETARY OF NAVY.

Naval Chiefs.

I.

INTREPID seamen! patriots! men
    Triumphant in your earlier day!
Valor, without steel armor, then
Brought fame to fleets that slow decay;
Your tried successors still achieve
With mail-clad squadrons deeds sublime;
While fair hands heroes' chaplets weave,
Whose names adorn the scroll of Time!

    Unfailing Science called to aid,
Compliant lent her mighty arm;
To victory paths for prowess made,
Unscath'd still strove through Ruin's storm!

    Augment their conquering forces vast!
O'er seas the Nation's bound'ry grows!

To-day her names pale not by those,
The grand old masters of the past!

Let Traffic's argosies expand,
Brisk Commerce, 'neath protection's sway,
Revive along Columbia's strand,
And swift Progression's call obey:
Let Ocean's tributes be our own,
Which long to rival shores have flown:

To emulate! to still aspire!
As each the place of power assumes,
To raise the sea's proud standard higher,
As each the Navy's Chief becomes,
Let his aim be to works repeat,
That grace the Secretary's seat:

For, while Muscovy's wily Tzar
Bids "Peace," make all the nations glad,
All wary wait on "Adam Zad!"
Whose fleets and armies growing are,
Still red Mars rolls his fiery car,
While Time yet makes no end to war!

III.

Long swift assembled on the sea
While strife o'er tropic waters spread,
Fleets by gallant Commanders led
Against the wily enemy!
Who ever-conquering standards bore
Along the farthest ocean shore!
Whose bold exploits applause would wring
From every realm, each despot king!

The Secretary's mind was train'd
Through busy action's varied scenes,—
Well drill'd, well school'd; wise course maintain'd
Till varied gifts high place sustain'd;
Till gather'd store of legal lore,
That to things nautical pertain'd,
Rich fruits exalted genius bore,
His present proud position gain'd,—
Which studious past had taught to fill
With art consummate, tactful skill!

IV.

Advisors eminent stood nigh,
Whose forceful minds' impact was felt;
Aides, ALLEN, FINNEY, ROOSEVELT,
Whose apt resources plans supply,
Meet prompt each near emergency!

Head of the Sea's Department great,
Sustain'd was in his wid'ning field
By NEPTUNE's train'd triumvirate,
MAHAN, SICARD, skill'd CROWNINSHIELD:
For, older conflicts, many seas
Taught these experienc'd men; and these,
By Ocean school'd, well in accord,
Fail'd ne'er to priceless aid afford,
The war's most prescient Naval Board!

V.

The tireless ROOSEVELT was there,
Ere San Juan heard his war-cry ring!
To well prepare, with LONG to share,
The vast Department's heavy care,
Place men, fleets, posts, scan everything!

HON. THEODORE ROOSEVELT, GOVERNOR OF NEW YORK.
AUTHOR, SOLDIER, STATESMAN.

NAVAL CHIEFS.

Strong figure picturesque is he,
Destined a varied fame to find,
Phenomenal in energy,
Leader, in every sense defin'd!
At Hong Kong's port placed vast supplies
Should need, perchance, therefor arise:
Foreseeing war with prophet's eyes,
Far-reaching, bold, resourceful mind!

On him, wherever seen or heard,
Ever is firmest trust conferr'd;
Well earn'd, nor yet by him betray'd
In forum, field, where're array'd;
Whose oratory's graces charm,
Whose thoughts, in clear conviction's train,
Logic in phrase concise maintain,
Bid list'ners right convictions form:

His earnest nature stirred, deep wrought
By whate'er theme secures his thought,
His realistic pen makes plain,
In volumes with acumen fraught,

"Ideals" high strong souls attain,—
In trenchant style, strong, clear, concise,
High attributes all readers prize:

Some years were spent in ventures' quest,
As ranchman, helping "Win the West:"
Tales, from bold huntsmens' wild haunts came,
That stir the blood, of "Noble Game!"
From war return'd, high honors won,
Truth through his polished pages shone:

VI.

Wherever posts of great trust call'd
That right stood with him all confest;
And if at times his justice gall'd,
Integrity his acts imprest:

While toiling up the hill of **Fame**,
Engaged in service national,
State, army, place municipal,
From each post fill'd at duty's call,
Strong words commendatory came:

NAVAL CHIEFS. 67

For rank nor place; bribe, howe'r strong,
Would he conceal, connive at wrong:

In whate'er school of life engaged,
Research supplies rich mental stores;
Through records delved of naval wars,
As his work there events presaged;
To whom historian's duties fall,
Acquiring knowledge technical
That, at his country's need, availed
Him well who on such store could call
When the land's armor'd squadrons sailed!

VII.

Let Santiago's scenes attest,
Him battle's horrors ne'er appall'd;
That fear bode never in his breast,
Leading his charge! Death everywhere!
Inspiring men, his constant care,
Dashing, enthusiastic, bold!
Well bravery's medal was decreed,
Well-won his General's stars, indeed!

The Colonel of the Riders Rough,
Though made of firm, heroic stuff,
Might not from kindly deed forbear,
Whose State failed not such past to scan:
From statesmen sage, heroic men,
Chose him to grace her Governor's chair!
And those well versed in parties said:
'T was sure defeat, unless he led
The combin'd hosts who placed him there!

ADMIRAL GEORGE DEWEY, U. S. N.

Heroes of the Spanish-American War.

PART THIRD.

Dewey.

I.

COMMODORE DEWEY cruised along
    Warm shores where Asia's islands are;
His fleet assembling, staunch and strong,
At Hong Kong's port, where busy stir
Munitions drew from waiting store,
Destruction's food, huge guns supplies,
Rumors of war had sent him for!
Convey'd on board 'neath watchful eyes,

That probe all things, close scrutinize;
Till battle's gray his cruisers o'er,—
The hue of Ocean seen from far,—
Completes their panoply of war!

Here Dwyer, with the Baltimore,
Hurries from Japan's neighboring shore,
The fighting force augmenting more:

Britain to treat, with court'sy meet,
These cousins, this sojourning fleet,
Extends warm sympathetic hand;
Bids welcome to the Eastern strand;
Prepares reception, concert, fête,
Forgetting every ancient feud.
Prospective neighbors well to greet,
Whose coming means the common good.

II.

These Western Giants, hand-in-hand,
From Albion's isle, Columbia's strand,
Bid civilization's fostering ray
O'er Earth's benighted regions play!

Two sister cities, two fair isles,
Each looking o'er her beauteous bay,
Basking in Orient's dimpling smiles,
Redeemed from mediæval sway,
That like a pall above them lay.
Now hail progression's bright'ning day!

* * * * * * *

* * * * * * *

III.

HONG KONG! Glad isle of "Fragrant Streams,"
Where Chu Kiang's broad current pours,
High basking in the tropic beams,
Where Britain o'er Celestial shores
Advances still with march sublime,
Where dominates her widening claims
The unschool'd tribes of Asia's clime:

Loom stern-brow'd mountains, serried, dark,
Whose pictur'd crags deep tides repeat
In blue waves dimpling at their feet,
Which far at sea glad seamen mark!

Bright, on the north shore, gem of all,
Fair sits the festive Capital
Of this bold isle, once China's own,
By Britain ruled, advanced, rich grown:

IV.

Victoria! High your splendors lie
In picturesque magnificence,
Where terrac'd slopes ascending vie,
Whose startling contrasts please each sense:
Rude hills round beauteous gardens bend,
Where Art's fair shapes with Nature's blend;
With galleries high, imposing stand
Academy, bourse, palace grand,
Spectacular on every hand!

Thus Progress, to high purpose dear,
Contrasting strange to Western eye,
O'er Orient's frailer structures nigh,
Would her enduring models rear:

Pacific's varied products lure
Good ships that throng from many a shore,

That anchor'd here may ride secure,
When torrid tempests threat'ning roar!

  South side the isle, some leagues between,
At Koo Loo's docks, at Aberdeen,
Sea-sanitariums vast equip,
Restore and cure each crippled ship,
Pursued by typhoon's rage to seek
Safe anchorage 'neath the giant peak:

V.

  Her harbor wide is stirring scene!
All crafts that breast the tropic gale
In this port Commerce bids convene;
From frailest shell to ship of steel,
Propell'd by ocean-buried screws;
Impell'd by wheel, all types of sail,
Shoulder-of-mutton, mat, latteen;
Out-riggers, South-Sea carv'd canoes;
Junks, cruisers, proas—strange array!
Fleets from the Suez water-way!
Rowed, paddled, sculled by swarthy crews,
Aggressive here to mart their store;

Here mingle tribes of motley hues,
By Asia's yellow race supplied,
From Shanghai's, Yokohama's shore,
Bombay, Calcutta, Singapore;
Malaysians, like the olive dyed,
Manilamen of tawny shade;
Bay Mongols, Anglo-Saxons pale,
Tribes that along the "Straits" abide,
Whose Babled tongues the ear assail;
Who when on land are less at ease
Than when on boats or plung'd in seas!

VI.

Where arts municipal attest
The high ideals of the West,
Here Albion grasps Columbia's hand,
Gives cordially fraternal aid;
Bids her enlighten'd sway extend,
Her staunch fleet welcomes to her strand,
So soon to hostile realms invade!

Aye, speed yon fleet that rides below!
Whose Captains train'd, whose men of skill

Prepare to meet a boasting foe,
Momentous mission to fulfil;
To mighty, far-spread change effect,
He who commands would scarce suspect,
Southeastward o'er the China sea,
Ere long in broad Manila Bay,
By shores two hundred leagues away!

    * * * * * * * *
    * * * * * * * *

VII.

As Hong Kong's Governor's neutral law
No longer might allow delay,
'T was meet the fleet at once withdraw
From thence:
         Some leagues they bore away
Where up the coast contiguous lay
China's convenient port, Mirs Bay;
Where cutter, Hugh McCulloch, brought
News that most startling import bore,—
Orders that thrill'd the Commodore!
His crews enthus'd, who keenly sought
For actual war!

These orders greet:
"Capture, destroy the Spanish fleet!"
With lips stern set, with countenance firm,
With look that presag'd battle's storm,
Foreshadowing destiny!

Said he,
While burn'd the lightning in his glance,
Remem'bring the Maine's tragedy:
"Thank the Lord! Now, I've got the chance,
I'll wipe them from the Sea's expanse!"
And order'd prompt his fleet's advance!

VIII.

Historic, fateful first of May!
A nation bursts its bonds! The hour,
The cause brings forth the man of power!
DEWEY must meet, the coming day,
MONTOJO in Manila Bay!

Should Spain triumph what gloom would lower!
For rendezvous her fleets would go

DEWEY.

To Honolulu's open port
Pacific's commerce cutting short;
From far Yukon to Mexico,
Laying the west coast cities low!

   Fort Fisher, red Donaldsonville
LIEUTENANT DEWEY soundly taught,—
Experience gave, developed skill,
School'd by immortal Farragut;
Successor his high rank to fill,—
Whose victory Admiral's pennant won!
One of the Mississippi's men,
Who showed true hero's spirit when
He that shot-riddled ship stood on
As she 'neath bomb-torn waves went down,
The struggling crew about him strewn!

IX.

   Commander made, by many a shore
His cruisers scour'd the oceans o'er:
On land, on sea, serv'd double score
Of years, which vast experience bore:

Unflinching, cool and careful when
The stir and whirl of quick events
Confuse the man of weaker sense,
With mind direct, practical, plain:

Shall statesman's mantle fall on him?
What germs of power unfolded be,
Hid in that ancient parent tree,
That bears full many a fruitful limb
Of enterprising pedigree?

Typical Yankee through and through,
Let old Montpelier's annals show
What forces bade ambition grow,—
Where ETHAN ALLEN, sternly great,
From marble in her Hall of State,
Called on the youth to emulate!

His sire objected to the sea,
But when the instinct native be,
Declares the Book of Destiny,—
His right vocation, soon or late,
Shall find the man high deeds await!

THE OLYMPIA, ADMIRAL DEWEY'S FLAGSHIP.

The Asian Squadron.

I.

THE fleet, for Luzon's restless isle,
  Breasted six hundred miles of wave,
A scornful enemy to foil;
With cruisers manned by seamen brave,
To rend from Spain's remorseless hand
This fruitful realm, this Eden strand:

  The dread typhoon forgets its rage,
The sea and sky mild aspect wear;
Each boist'rous surge soft winds assuage,
Light zephyrs fan the sultry air,
Stray drifting, fleece-like clouds appear,
While heavens smile; blue waves beguile;
Spirits of combat waft them where,

THE ASIAN SQUADRON.

With morn's first watch, shall rage the while
Destruction thund'ring o'er the isle!

To crush MONTOJO's fleet nor lack
In eye and hand, nor cunning lose,
To frequent drills were piped the crews,
As now no monsoons cross'd their track:

'T is true as trite, his work is best,
Whose faculties rust not with rest:
The fight to come is to be won
By practis'd men behind each gun!

II.

All honor to the gunner tried,
Whose courage high none may assail;
Though his ship through thick battle ride,
Laughs 'mid war's furious iron hail,
That 'round him falls without avail!
Steadfast in action, at his post,
Deck, hold, top, turret,—till life fail,
By duty bound, at whate'er cost,—
His country's flag his proudest boast!

THE ASIAN SQUADRON.

Where are more skilful seamen found
Than cruise beneath the stripes and stars?
Go, search the wide sea's utmost bound,
Match the White Squadron's gallant tars!
Though few as yet their battle scars,
Annihilation's order given:
"Cast loose! Provide!" strife's spirit stirs,
Till, by unerring volleys driven,
Sink the foe's ships asunder riven!

JACK is at duty's call alert,
Array'd fastidious, bold and free;
Careless of forms, strange yarns divert,
Heard, spun or read of land or sea;
Love, friendship true, integrity
Sheet-anchor form of seamen's breast;
While these faults rule, if faults they be,
Where ship's bounds action's lines invest,
Where careless heart makes life a jest,
Salutes a maid nor need be prest!

* * * * * * *
* * * * * * *

V.

When Boliano's Point was nigh,
Southward the squadron bent its way,—
A long, slow-moving line of gray,—
Where Luzon's shores enchanting lie:

The elements were more than kind,
Good omen therefrom well divined;
Unchanged, till broad Manila Bay
Was scarce one brief day's cruise away:

To find the fleet of Montojo—
Lest Spain's wiles leave them in the lurch,—
Three scouting cruisers went to search
Those neighboring ports, Boliano
And Subic Bay:
     Returned they show
No trace was found of any foe:

VI.

The squadron hugs the tropic shore
By rich-hued foliage flaunting gay,
To feast the ravished eye the more,

Beguile the sultry, lingering day;
Where vine-clad harbors shade the sea
Wave balmy groves; while Ocean's breeze
Wafts spicy odors from the lea
O'er jutting rocks and tropic trees,
Cool glens, romantic scenery:

Poet or painter never drew
A fairer, more inviting scene!
In settings of all shades of green,
Blending in brilliant, varying hue,
With flowers of every gorgeous dye,
That intersect and multiply
The panoramic view moves by!

From out this flame of bloom and leaf,
Wild Nature's wealth of solitude,
A thousand tempting fruits protrude,
Sculptured in picturesque relief:

VII.

Beautiful island of Luzon!
Little do your shorn people know

What new existence now dawns on
Their hapless lives:

                Hard by, e'en now,
Invulnerable, his cruisers glide
Whose coming marks your fateful day:
Then, make that starry flag your pride,
Your madness meets in arm'd array!

VIII.

  Dewey brings Aguinaldo famed,
Bestows his powerful fleet's relief,
Assists the Phillipino Chief,
'Till his loved isles shall be reclaimed,
Pledged with his followers to aid
His new ally, for strife arrayed:

  With ruthless Spain the Chief had fought,
Her promise forced for juster rule;
Then, by her snare insidious caught,
He found himself the spoiler's tool!
Till now, no more her word beguiles,
Matched Dewey's guns 'gainst Spanish wiles:

By Hong Kong's Consul's generous plan
Convey'd back to his strug'ling isles!

Alas, that e'er ambitions vain
Should with delusions fire the brain
Of this rude child of Asia's plain:
Cajoled by that designing band,
Progression's foes in Freedom's land,
Strife fost'ring 'neath obstruction's hand,
Till blood again must stain the sand,
Ilolio's isle, Manila's strand!

VIII.

As Consul, WILDMAN went before
This war its hostile fleets arrayed
Securing facts:
          At Singapore,
To represent the land delayed;
Whose prescience for the strife prepared,
Vast knowledge gaining much desired,
Of harbor depths, the lay of land;
Facts that to fleets and forts pertend

That the Commander then requir'd,
Of insurrectionary schemes,—
A long array of useful themes!

   The Consul had through Borneo strayed,
Strange races brought from tropic shore
That thronged Chicago's Fair arrayed:
Fruits energetic research bore.
That all the World was marveling o'er!

   Commissioned 'mong half-savage chiefs
With customs strange, despotic reign,
He could such friendly aid obtain
This tactful man alone receives,
Who well tales of those days relates
Passed 'mong the dwellers of the "Straits:"

IX.

Ere torrid climes he learned to know,
Each untried way before him lay,
He taught the living page to glow
Where California ope'd the way;
When *Overland* sought noted men,

Sought humorous TWAIN'S, BRET HARTE'S
  quaint pen:
And now, in middle-manhood's prime,
Fame points the way and bids him climb!

  Manhattan's isle had given him birth,
And sent his youthful spirit forth
'Mong torrid nations of the earth;
On him who thence rare treasures brought
Smithsonian's Sons of Science sought
Associate's honors to bestow;
Whose purpose high naught should abate
Till Hong Kong's Consul General's brow
The years shall laurel with the great!

CAPT. JOSEPH B. COGHLAN,
OF THE CRUISER RALEIGH, U. S. N.

By courtesy of Leslie's Weekly.

The Cruisers' Captains.

I.

OFF shore the fleet rides calmest seas,
  Waiting till evening spreads her pall,
While signals flaunt in fitful breeze
Announcing that the Admiral,
Now close upon the Spaniard's track,
His captains all to council call;
To plan near battle's prompt attack,
Convinced in land-locked waters near
The enemy must soon appear!

 Success meant everything next day,
Dread ruin certain in defeat,
When all supplies, with succor meet,
Were full six thousand miles away!

The sea-dogs staunch the flag-ship board,
Each face by long experience scored
'Neath scorching suns; on sea and land
Well seam'd and tann'd; by salt winds fann'd;
Minds with much sea-gain'd wisdom stored,
Sojourns in port, on wave afford:

Each man the dauntless spirit owns
Of Perry, Foote, Decatur, Jones;
And well their country may bestow
Honors where such high merits glow!

To these men is the glory due,
Commanders in Manila's fight,
Backed by their guns and seamen true,
With those who, shut from sight and light,
Sent war's munitions from below,
Like Gunner Evans' motley crew:

II.

Chief-of-Staff Captain Lamberton,
Whose plans shrewd tho't, quick wit preserve,
Whose ready hand and steady nerve

Bid him on the Olympia serve,
Is Pennsylvania's genial son:

A mighty NIMROD when on shore,
Rejoices 'mid the cannons' roar!
Of many a task he e'en could tell,
Requiring tact, consummate skill,
The service had called him to fill:

After the Spaniard's flag was low
LAMBERTON went with WOOD, that day,
On shore, inside Cavité's bay,
To take surrender from the foe.

III.

The Flag-Ship's gallant Captain came
From Erie's shore, where PERRY's fame
Still lingers, and whose prowess great
Such souls as GRIDLEY's emulate;
Whose skill Manila saw maintain
His well-won name for pluck and brain;
Mark'd by full many a sterling trait
The true advisor indicate:

He at the Admiral's order sought
The tower from which his ship was fought;
Manœuvering the Olympia well,
The Captain made each battery tell!
Whose last broadside showed power to think
That made Montjo's Flag-Ship sink!

Alas, for latest honors won,
Was scarcely passed life's glorious noon
When Death the hero made his own:
His grand career closed all too soon,
Round whom Fame's sun of promise shown!
She who was left at home to mourn,
Expecting soon his glad return,
Her children of fond father shorn,
Receives but ashes and his urn.

IV.

O'er Dwyer of the Baltimore,
Annapolis never held control;
'Mid rude strife taught, wild breakers' roar,
He claims Old Ocean for his school!

Captain and ship, well-mated twain,
More gallant pair ne'er rode the Main!
Both proved their lessons mastered well
Amid Cavité's fiery hell!

V.

COGHLAN commands the Raleigh's crew
Who sent the first shot 'mid the foe,
Passing dark Boca Grandé through:
Tried seaman! Is there danger e'er
Shall cause that soul to shrink with fear!

To wit, to genial arts inclined,
Most sturdy opponent is he
At wordy fence and repartee;
Who knows well how to speak his mind,—
Thorough tactician of the sea!

VI.

While CAPTAIN WALKER'S past should claim
High place for him 'mong men of fame;
And though Annapolis praised his name,
Instructor most judicious, wise,

'T was on the Concord greatness came
Amid Manila's hail and flame!
Where shone exalted qualities
Of born commander, bound to rise!

   The Admiral knew well his man,
And when Manila's fight began,
The Flag-Ship with the Concord poured
Shot from the guns that foremost roared!

   While the fleet at Manila lay,
After its first victorious fray,
Raleigh and Concord steamed away
To stay the German cruiser's sway,
And seized Spain's forts at Subic Bay!

VII.

Ohio's son, the veteran WOOD,
Bold Captain of the Petrel! stood
Nearest Cavité's forts next day
Amid the batteries' fiercest play!
With devastating broadside-blows
Still'd the last guns at battle's close!

There ne'er was more hilarious soul,
When thund'ring guns began to roll,
Than SKIPPER HUGHES, of fighting blood,
Who shouts, while shrieking shells explode,
"By heavens! This looks like business, WOOD!"

VIII.

WILDES, Captain of the Boston, comes
From Old Bay State's ancestral homes,
Whose ancient annals quaintly trace
His Revolutionary race:

There might be something said of tea
By strong-soul'd men thrown in the sea,
Which tale fits other time and place:

The Boston's Captain's heart was light,
Near mid-day, in Cavité's fight,
When steaming toward the inside bay
To sieze those ships that therein lay,
Where, 'mid shells' crash and roar of gun,
His cruiser well her honors won!

✻ ✻ ✻ ✻ ✻ ✻ ✻

IX.

The Captains, by the Admiral
Convened, are in his cabin; here,
Ere eve her pall shall spread o'er all,
Elaborating with strict care,
Manœuvers for a dawn attack!
That each in time may be aware,
Of the bold plan, his part prepare,
When he conveys the glad news back
To men who man each giant gun,
By whom the battle must be won!
Whose cheer is like the charger's neigh,
That scents the battle far away!

Intrepid men these seamen are,
From Admiral to able tar,
Disciplined e'en to finger tips
To men command, work guns or ships,
All eager for the stir of war!

COL. JOHN HAY,
SECRETARY OF STATE AND EX-AMBASSADOR TO GREAT BRITAIN.

Heroes of the Spanish-American War.

PART FOURTH.

War's Leviathans.

I.

THE gallant line the Flag-Ship leads
  Of cruisers that majestic glide,
Whose whirling blades Old Ocean feeds,
Impelling through the Sea's smooth tide
Ships that in colder waters bide;
With powers destructive chained that go
O'er the abyss in strength and pride,
Passing Pacific's billows through,
While long swells yield like drops of dew:

That glorious flag floats o'er each deck,
The stars and stripes of liberty!
That standard sheet, that o'er the wreck
Of baffled Spain her isles shall free
When Freedom's sons win victory!
Called to redeem the Eastern World,
The Orient land, the tropic sea,
In each zone, warm or cold, unfurled,
Defiance toward Oppression hurled!

II.

Nine staunch ships DEWEY's squadron form,
Manned by Columbia's sturdy sons;
Six cruisers!   Countless glittering tons
Of war's destructive engines arm
Their bristling ports!   Tremendous guns,
The turret's monsters!   Death's machines!
Dread "secondaries'" tubes portend;
Each Gatling wholesale slaughter means!
Ingenious rapid-firers stand

Where they the foe's deck best command;
In fighting-tops guns downward trend,
While arms of varying caliber
Hurl shot, shell, schrapnel wide and far!

III.

Here Science finds the faultless range,
Which logarithms must calculate:
Whence reasoning, is it ever strange
The enemy should find defeat
Who bade his cruisers doom'd advance,
Relying on the wildest chance?
Invade that line-of-battle's flame
Whose accurate volleys never fail,
Annihilation's withering gale!
Guns leveled to precision's aim,
Applied mechanics tell the tale!

IV.

Here dominates triumphant Art,
The strong, subdued Colossus sways;
Each impulse of the throbbing heart

The master's hand impells or stays,
Extended:
   At his touch or sign,
Where fires Plutonian raging glow,
Where iron nerves enmazed combine
'Mid hot, volcanic depths below,
Throats 'neath restrain'd exertion pant,
The monster tamed, made suppliant!

V.

 Here sentient brain, puissant soul,
Mind, guides the living, moving whole;
Along a myriad devious ways,
The harness'd forces rules with ease;
Each nerve far-stretching Thought obeys,
That everywhere compells control
From bow to stern, top-mast to keel;
From Ocean-buried whirling wheel,
O'er every gleaming muscle's steel!

 Each shape Cyclopean breasts the seas,
Teeming with life, inspiring awe;

With emblem streaming in the breeze
Proclaiming prosperous reign of law!

From plucky Petrel, small but sound,
Of pending storm the herald, same
As omen'd fowl whence comes her name;
To grand Olympia, turret-crown'd,
Named from the mount of classic fame—
To crush the lurking Spaniard bound,
Where're his squadron may be found!

VI.

The cutter, Hugh McCulloch, bears
Dispatches, when the need appears;
And, later on, the trip makes short
To Hong Kong's most convenient port;
Commission'd for her swift lines neat,
The messenger to serve the fleet:

The conflict HODGSON fain would share,
On whose deck guns aggressive show,
Yet must in rear of fighters steer;
After whom laden colliers go,

The Nanshan and the Zafiro.
Purchased through DEWEY's keen foresight
And prescient suggestion rare,
Abundant fuel to prepare
At need to have convenient there,
After the near impending fight;
During which these shall ride serene,
While fighting cruisers intervene.
Fierce battling with the foe between!

HON. LYMAN J. GAGE,
SECRETARY OF THE TREASURY.

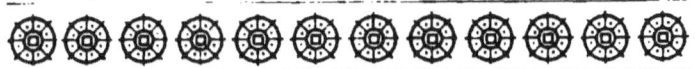

The Eve of Battle.

I.

NIGHT'S shadows greet the waiting fleet,
　　With crews alert, all things complete,
That, armed by Fate, defies defeat!
To strike a blow that shall resound
The circumambient globe around!

　Though the brief list is not so long
As the Greek ships of HOMER's song,
Incomparably more staunch and strong!

　For, arts of war, undreamed of then,
Since Science now has part to play,
With many a force unknown to men
In AGAMEMNON's, HECTOR's day,
Now metamorphose battle's plan.

II.

In the Olympia's cabin sat
The Admiral and Captains all,
Discussing each manœuver that
To battle's shifting needs should fall;
Till all expedients were scanned,
Adapted to the methods planned,
Whate're should be the action's trend:

Soon each must readiness avouch,
Prepared for combat's near approach,
While each man's ship, all points minute,
Engaged the Leader's mind acute!

Verity went with DEWEY's word,
Who well knew how that race deferred:
"To Spaniard, haste is 'kin to crime,
Manaña is his favorite time!—
Strike before day, shall be my way,
Disturbing him in his delay,
Ere he prepares!"
     His Captains go
Manila's bay to soon invade,

THE EVE OF BATTLE.

With details laid for midnight's raid,
When night's shield hides them from the foe;
When sleepy sentries steal below,
Whose lights gleam from Corregidor,
And which they must unnoticed pass,
To well insure the fleet's success.

At day's decline the crews the while,
Sent many a soul-inspiring strain
From horn and viol o'er the main;
With music, song the hour beguile,
For this brief respite fain to turn
From battle's preparations stern!

III.

The sun sinks down the purpling west,
Flames on the bosom of the deep;
The waves, in sapphire fringes drest,
In gentlest undulations sweep:
Soft twilights' shades o'er Ocean creep,
As last beams fade of solar fire;
Gulls nestle on the wave asleep,

Fishes to coral caves retire,
Heaven dons resplendent night's attire:

How beautiful is night at sea,
When naught obscures the vaulted sky!
Whose dome hung with blue drapery,
Blends with horizon's azure dye:
Lights living, burning meet the eye
Above, around: The deeps below,
Like turquoise pavement, seem to vie
With heaven: The seas flash to and fro,
Each wave one starry, spangled glow!

Tumbling around the vessels play
Shoals of huge grampus in the surge;
Blowing the seas in fiery spray,
As from the waters they diverge,
On waves disport, anon submerge;
Fluking, as plunging they subtend,
With fan-spread tails the low swells scourge,
As monsoons that o'er mountains bend,
Lash hills that round Luzon's shores trend!

IV.

The booby on the quarter-rail
Sleeps, staid in his uncertain flight
By canvas white in evening's gale,
Like late fly lured by taper's light:
As day declines, night's shades prevail,
Wings weary way along the sea,
And heedless falls on net or sail
That meets his eye: for naught cares he,
Cruiser, trader or pirate free,
As one 'mid care falls helplessly.

So the worn wanderer insecure
Sleeps when Night finds him in the wild;
By *ignis fatuous'* faithless lure
Led blindly on. like thoughtless child,
Chasing fire-fly in evening mild;
Through bog. marsh, tangled copse pursues
His dubious way, with mire defiled,
Till drooping nature fails to choose,
Sinking 'mid dangers, damps and dews,
While black Night's curtains round him close.

V.

Fair Cynthia rides upon the wave,
Disporting there with calm delight:
From caves with coral architrave
Mermaids rise in the radiance bright,
That from her train of silver light,
Commingles with the restless billow;
The Hours sleep on the lap of Night,
Fann'd by winds whisp'ring round their pillow,
As murmuring land-breeze stirs the willow.

HON. JOHN W. GRIGGS, OF NEW JERSEY,
ATTORNEY-GENERAL.

Passing the Boca Grande.

I.

THE first night-watch had just come on,
And evening's stillness settled down,
When bugle's blair harsh rent the air!
Quick gliding up and down each mast,
To every ship the signal passed—
Red lights and white flashed everywhere!

Stood on his bridge the Admiral,
Whose standard the Olympia shall
Bare through the coming battle's pall!

"Prepare for action!" Quick response!
His searching glance beholds advance
His ship's half-thousand; at that call
All cruisers' crews obey at once!

II.

Each man springs to his well-known post,
And all unnecessary things
Into the sea remorseless flings,
To be like vagrant wreckage tost:

Superfluous "diddy-boxes" go,
With many a treasured curio
That seems to some like fortune lost,
Enriching that most thankless coast:

'Neath axes sharp of brawny tars,
Wood-work and ornamental gear
Like magic fall and disappear
With useless sails and extra spars:

While crews enthuse with life and stir
No need has GRIDLEY to defer:
"Ready the ship for action, Sir!"

The squadron's brave Commander, glad,
Knowing the gallant men he had,
With each trim ship for battle stripped—
Noting how prompt each was equipped,

As calm they rode the shadowy brine—
Stood looking down the moon-lit line:

III.

The Admiral dwells not in gloom,
Whose place, demeanor scarce allow
Approach from those who much assume;
Whose well-poised head, commanding brow
Give highest purpose ample room;
And few would pass the veteran by
Nor mark that keenly piercing eye!

He views with scorn all dangers born,
Encountered ere by land or sea;
Nor from his acts is caution shorn
Who plans exploits most carefully,
And, well prepared, waits battle's morn:

Like men the Great NAPOLEON chose
To honor with Field-Marshal's place,
Somewhat the Roman type of nose
Gives character to that strong face,
That shows some lines of care of late;

Where, vigilant, 'tis his to wait
Long tedious months, nor care abate,
While his will guides a people's fate!

IV.

Genius—with many a sterling trait,
Link'd with impressive moral force,
That shapes of great events the course—
Conspires this hero to create,
Whose kindliness of heart has won,
And made the whole command his own:

On quarter-deck, wherever tried,
Truth, mercy, justice guide his will;
The careful judge, true seaman still,
Who leans e'er toward the weaker side:

When lighter themes his thoughts engage,
He mingles in, with equal zest,
The social swim or battle's rage,
Scarce passed as yet life's middle stage;
Whose friends have everywhere confest.
They loved him most who knew him best!

THE BOCA GRANDE.

Precise the Admiral is, exact;
Better possess'd these traits than lack'd
By one Fate stamps, with firmest hand,
With that born genius to command;
Traits that exalt the Freeman o'er
The proudest high-throned Emperor!

V.

Oft had he rode the mountain wave
Up-rear'd by tempest's howling blast,
That gored the deep with many a grave,
That—by mad elements dug—aghast
Yawn'd o'er the waters, while the mast
Bent to the charging winds that roar
The Ocean's wrath! The foaming vast
His frighten'd barque went reeling o'er,
Driving toward the rock-reef'd shore!

At morn he shall direct the strife,
Driving the foe to helpless woe,
His ships dismantl'd! Left but life,
With boastful pride prostrated low,

The crews of Spain, of MONTOJO,
Shall honors, station, fame forego:
The victor wins in strife's red hour—
When, tripple-wing'd, hurl'd to and fro,
Death hurtles, shrieking to devour—
Gifts highest in his country's dower!

 * * * * * * *
 * * * * * * *

VI.

THE sky grew dark: A heavy cloud,
That fell o'er Nature like a shroud,
No ray from moon or star allow'd:

The squadron starts the channel through,
Steams fast in silent, lightless line:
Though guiding lights astern shall shine,
Hoods next the foe hide these from view:

There reigns a spell of fierce suspense
That holds each officer and crew:
With each nerve strain'd, keen-set, intense,
While dangers threat, unseen, immense,
Imminent doom thrills every sense!

THE BOCA GRANDE.

Suspended o'er destruction's brink,
On any deck, perchance, may drop
Huge missile thrown from thund'ring Krupp
That might their still procession stop!

Guns yawn that could each cruiser sink;
Sprung mine might stay the line's advance,
Leaving for each life slender chance!

VII.

The last ship comes unchalleng'd clear,
Has Boca Grande safely pass'd;
As to arrest such unsought guest
A loud boom shakes the startled air
Whose shot plows waters in the rear!

The Hugh McCulloch's tell-tale spark
Burning against the heavens dark,
Her cinders flaming through the sky,
Proclaim the fleet is stealing by!

Incautious firemen down below,
Feeding the roaring furnace glow,
Have, inadvertent, warned the foe!

Rockets flash'd o'er Corregidor
Bring answer from the northern shore!
While land-guns multiply their roar,
Whose lingering shots fall never near:

Raleigh, Concord, Boston return
Reply to these alarms astern,
Delinquent in their waken'd wrath;
While DEWEY seeks his lurking prey
Hard by Manila, leagues away,
Signaling all to join his path:

VIII.

The Boca passed, each weary tar
Sleeps by his waiting dog of war,
When earliest dawn succeeds the dark,
To open loud with deep-toned bark!

Crews crowd the fires, each furnace glows,
Huge engines scalding fumes evolve;
Steam hissing toils in dying throes,
As 't would its iron bands resolve!
The living forces fierce convolve,

Pant for vent! Valves alternate play,
Pent power escapes! Strong screws revolve,
Urging each vessel through the spray,
Speed doubling o'er the dangerous way!

IX.

Through waters dark and treacherous, fast
Cruising above that stranger wave,
As many a league the squadron pass'd,
The Flag-Ship's navigator gave
Forth powers of highest human skill!

Alert and careful, CALKINS still
Along Death's vale of shade progress'd,
Though bravest here might shrink by day!
Now, through black night, no ray reveal'd,
These dare this mine-infested field,
Paved with destruction!
      Dangerous way!
No beacon light, with judgment fine,
Defying shoal and hidden mine,
Conquering the demons of the brine!

What signs of fray?
                    Deep in the bay,
Half-hid by mists of morning gray,
An unknown fleet before them lay!

   Are these those ships, MONTOJO's boast,
Toward which they steer?
                    Traders are these,
Staid merchantmen, the ships of peace,
Moor'd safe along the guardian coast
Where flags of all lands fan the breeze,
By earliest morn's damp vapors tost:

   Aurora's tints scarce gild the deep,
Whose bosom waits Sol's soothing ray:
Warm winds, wak'd from their midnight sleep,
Herald, e'er long, the King of Day
To find the bay in fierce affray
Of thund'ring fleets, and war's alarm
Spread far and wide, above, midway!
Fierce as when torrid tempests arm
The raging monsoon's mighty storm!

PHILIPPINO LADY, OF MANILA.
SPANISH MESTIZO.

Manila.

I.

AS Dewey's fleet came o'er the bay,
 Dark waters rim in dawn's pale ray,
Manila's white walls dimly lay,
Backed by those mist-clad mountains gray,
The serried back-bone of Luzon:

Gay Venice 'neath an Orient sun!
On the isle's level south-west shore,
How fair the broad bay you look on,
Where ships of all lands throng your door!
Gone the harsh sway of fiendish tools,
Let Commerce grow, high enterprise,
And from your deadly thraldom rise!

* * * * * * *
* * * * * * *

II.

A TROPIC archipelago
Lies westward of the China Sea;
Eastward, Pacific's currents flow,
Southward, the waves of Celebé;
Southwestward stretch green island chains—
The Sulu and the Palawan—
'Twixt which the Sulu Sea flows on,
Where soft winds kiss the spicy plains
Fragrant with groves of cinnamon:

Southwest the coast Mindanio
Warm ocean-currents mingling flow
Between these isles and Borneo;
Where—seasons when the simoon roars—
Wild surges lash these storm-swept shores!

MAGELLAN, their discov'rer bold,
With PHILIP's name these islands curst,
Of all Spain's bigot kings the worst;
'Neath whose successors crimes untold,
Official scoundrels here have wrought;

The Philippino harass'd, bled,
Whose toil their greed insatiate fed;
While 'neath oppression's heavy foot,
Was crushed to earth each flower of thought,
While hate, long hid, low cunning bred.

III.

Like ocean-current, deep and strong,
A broad, resistless tidal force,
Eternal Progress, sweeps along,
Art, science following its course:

Enlighten'd Thought seeks Orient lands:
Through great events—Time's shifting sands—
Afar the Western life expands,
Whose ocean paths reach torrid shores,
While on the Star of Empire soars,
Where Commerce ope's to trade new doors!

The Western mind shall educate
These Malay tribes of varied hues;
Shall stronger elements infuse,
Bidding new vigor permeate,

A virile wakening elevate,
Stirred by a power naught can abate!

IV.

Ungrateful, much misguided race,
That rends the hand your welfare seeks,
Strange vent that long-pent hatred finds,
Which, now to generous motives blinds,
Through your proud Chief's ambition speaks!

Primitive methods must give place
To forms advanced high Art invents,
Born of an energy intense,
That shame your savage implements!
Wrought by the powerful Western hand,
To make of yours a prosperous land;
While equity's exchange shall share
With these productive islands fair!

For, lo, your gems of promise yield
To genius an inviting field,
And hither mighty fleets shall bear
All forms of civilization's ware;

MANILA.

For, fairer land sun shines not on
Than the rich region of Luzon!

V.

These isles of nutmeg, clove, bamboo
To Western eyes give pleasing view:
Forests indigenous and grand
Rise in profusion everywhere,
Where precious woods vast riches lend,
With countless products strange and new,
That rich and varied fruitage bear:

Here lives, companion to the palm,
The myriad-column'd banyan tree,
All arching from one parent stem,
That shelter for a town could be,
O'erspreading it entirely,
Well awning'd by the leafy hem:

VI.

Plants thrive with carnal qualities,
Whose leaves trap unsuspecting flies!
Exuding an adhesive wax,

Whose sweet the vagrant doom'd attracts;
Held by seductive honey here,
Unmindful of fast-binding powers,
Till the fierce plant its prey devours—
Giant Despair among the flowers!

So youth or maid, of careless air,
Heed fair designer's pleasing lure,
Held by soft charms seductive where
Intoxications banish care,
Till Reason holds her sway no more;
Insatiate pleasures all consume,
And life's best interests find a tomb.

VII.

Pineapple at Pana produced
Yields texture in fine garments used;
From which light fiber, wrought with skill,
Shawl of this gossamer pina will
The shell of walnut scarcely fill!

Embroid'rers rare designs invent
In ornamental yellow tint,

By Native girls' deft fingers wrought,
And by the wealthier classes sought:

'Mong fibrous plants that broadly grow
Banana yields a fibrous tow—
Manila's hemp the world supplies!
Here pleasing balm spreads, fragrant weed,
With all varieties of spice;
Rice, cocoa-plant, sweet aniseed—
Whence anisette's most cheering brew—
Vanila, coffee, indigo,
The sugar-cane's rich product, too!

Industrious in Nature's way,
These islanders vast skill display;
Whose marvelous genius will create
Most wondrous carvings intricate!

VIII.

Manila fair is pleasing scene,
Her river views and prospects gay
Recalling Adriatic's Queen;
Streets form'd by many a water-way,

MANILA.

Pasig, her Grand Canal; her bay,
Where traffic's busy precincts lay:

The Old Town sits shamed by the New,
Where Pasig's tides divide the twain:
Each low shore lined—most novel view!—
With Native huts, palm-thatch'd, bamboo;
While bridges picturesquely span—
Besides the Misericordia,
The Colganté and Ayola:

Inclosed by mediæval wall,
With draw-bridge, portcullis and moat,
Her ancient guns still point without,
Whose threatening mouths no foe appall!

IX.

Before the throng'd Entrada gate
Stretches Luenta's promenade;
Where, in her fairest garb array'd,
Manila walks and rides in state!
Or, all day's duties put aside,
This hour groups on the Prado ride:

Or thread Legazby's Avenue,
Named for the city's founder brave,
Who with Magellan plowed the wave;
Who first these fair isles came to know,
Savage and wild in tropic glow:

Here Philippino patriots died,
While passed by gorgeous pageants gay;
Shot down to make high holiday
For Spanish masters long defied!

X.

Music the Native dearly loves,
For, true musician born is he;
Whose unschool'd, unscor'd melody
The soul to each emotion moves:

His fighting-fowl, his dearest sport,
Is cherished with extremest care;
Smokes his cheroot, Manila rare—
Fowl, fruit and rice his chief support:

His scavenger the startling snake!
That in his garret's rafters dwells,

And rodents numerous expells,
Which rare repasts for saurians make!

To man this reptile harmless is,
Wer't not for which, like Hamelin, here
Good citizens would illy fare,
While these marauders marr'd their bliss!

XI.

His dwelling much is like the Swiss,
With many-gabled roof outside,
Where wide-projecting eaves provide
A cottage similar to his:

Novel effects within are spread
By many-hued glass globes o'erhead,
Whose blending shades are softly shed
From lamps which hang rich-color'd, gay:

A pale light filters lucid ray
Through thin pearl windows during day,
When opalescent light steals in
Through sea-shells made translucent, thin,
Fixed in light lattice planned to slide:

As windows serve, on every side
Adjust, admitting air within.

XII.

Manila's belle, the dark brunette,
Loves social life, gay dance and song;
Deck'd in her many-hued sarong,
Kind, charming, fascinating, yet:

Drap'd in fine textiles light as air,
Her rich, abundant raven hair
'Neath kerchief tasteful snooded 'round,
Falls rippling almost to the ground!

Fashion is to Manila's fair—
As to the soft sex everywhere—
Matter demanding skill and care;
Though, in her sultry, snowless clime,
Not clothed for warmth at any time!

She views the opera with delight,
And finds slight use for work or books:
In arts well skill'd enhancing looks,
That beautify and glad the sight:

With objects dear to woman's pride—
Cabinet neat, drest sideboard rare,
Carved intricate with marvelous care,
Glittering accessories here and there—
Her tasteful boudour is supplied:

Mother the husband must provide,
To her the suitor must propose!
The longings of his heart disclose;
Not seated by his charmer's side,
While fond eyes speak affection's pride
And honied discourse lingering flows.

* * * * * * *
* * * * * * *

Manila, high exalted be!
Glad San Miguel, Binondo blest;
Enroll'd with cities of the Free,
By their high spirit be imprest!
Like Venice throned, in beauty drest,
On Pasig's shores of verdure bright
Let Progress be your welcome guest,

MANILA.

Follow the Western Eagle's flight,
Soaring above the realms of Night!

Let your isles be like orbs that roll
About the vivid King of Day;
The Great Republic shall control
The destinies that mark their way!
Embryo States, behold them lay,
Link'd hand in hand! That flag unfurl'd,
Fades Mediæval twilight gray,
Falls on your shores Time's fost'ring ray;
Proud on Pacific's breezes curl'd,
Bright beacon of the Eastern World!

XIII.

Environ'd by deep bamboo bowers,
Rich bloom your tropic gardens fair;
Water'd and stirred by streams and showers,
Fann'd by spice-laden, perfum'd air:
Your Western guardian's generous care
Shall make your precincts pure as morn;
Learning shall fix her dwelling here,

And from broad minds high thoughts be born,
Whose products shall your life adorn!

  Art, Science, Genius here will bring
Their offerings of immortal birth;
When from your soil the germs shall spring,
Matured through men of sterling worth:
No more remote Columbia's shores,
Whose argosies spread o'er the earth,
Giving for products, precious ores,
The Western World's vast, varied stores.

    *   *   *   *   *   *   *
    *   *   *   *   *   *   *

XIV.

  COLUMBIA's Consuls honor'd stand,
To represent the Nation far;
Her exchange passing 'neath his hand,
Whose tact directs oft peace or war!
Whose province bids him recognize
Each venture sound that latent lies,
Inviting opportunities;
To show bold merchants many a prize

That in the path of commerce lies;
Whose consular reports are read—
Through the land's countless journals spread—
By stirring men of enterprise,
Shrewd sons of traffic through the land,
Aiding trade's channels to expand:

XV.

Shrewd, brainy men the service calls,
Minds with keen sense and judgment sound;
On whom oft task exacting falls—
Yet, when are these men wanting found?
Let countryman for justice call,
Let shipwreck'd crew meet sore distress:
Extending gurdianship to all,
Who need, find aid; the wrong'd, redress:

Since Freedom's fleets stern lesson taught,
The Consul at his foreign port
No longer looks on insult wrought,
Nor sees his flag the scoffer's sport,
Like CAPTAIN EVANS' gallant crew
Withstood at port of Callao!

XVI.

Williams, Manila's Consul wise,
Ere war's disturbing rumors came,
'Neath prying eyes of Spanish spies.
Prepared to meet strife's smould'ring flame,
So soon to rage 'neath tropic skies,
Whence should historic epoch rise!

Such task employed each leisure hour,
Inspecting arsenals and forts,
Probing Spain's hollow shell of power;
Whose Captains scoffed, in Eastern ports,
With sneers and shrugs and coarse retorts,
Boasting, their squadrons should devour,
The "Yankee Pigs" when war should lower!

The careful Consul yet contrived
To gain rich store of facts that bore
On hostile fleet and forts on shore,
Whence Dewey valued aid derived,
Passing Manila's waters through,
Whose untried depths therefrom he knew:

XVII.

The Consul saw insults deride,
When rights his countrymen would claim;
Yet must scorns unredress'd abide.
Though scarcely borne with spirit tame
By those forced 'neath his roof to ask
Protection:
        'Twas tactful task,
While oft rebelled his Freeman's pride
To see his country's rights defied!

The Nation's agent constant strove
The barb'rous tyrants' hands to stay,
If aught such ruthless souls might move,
Who made these Native tribes a prey;
Here slain by Spain, by tens, by scores,
Mured in low cells along the strand,
Insidiously designed so deep,
That when the high tide's current pours,
O'er drowning victims surges sweep;
While horror reigns throughout the land!

XVIII.

Williams anon saw wrongs redressed
By Dewey's guns' avenging flame!
Dons, who with haughty scorn confessed
Deep loathing for his country's name,
Hid their diminished heads in shame!
Through him begged intercession's claim—
Received at his hands many a boon,
Denied him in pride's prosperous noon:

Nor longer throng obtrusive spies,
Who here held reign 'neath barb'rous Spain—
Those harpies of the customs—ghouls
With horse-leech maw, ship-captains' bane!

LIEUT. THOMAS B. BRUMBY,

DEWEY'S FLAG-OFFICER, WHO HAD THE HONOR OF HOISTING THE AMERICAN FLAG AT MANILA, AUGUST 13, 1898.

Heroes of the Spanish-American War.

PART FIFTH.

Through Hostile Waters.

I.

IN the Olympia's wake, ere dawn,
The fleet steam'd north-east, then south, on
Till, some leagues from Manila's door,
The earliest twinkling morning star
Shone on the Spanish ships of war!
  Twelve vessels arm'd, all kinds, all told,
Wait confident in this stronghold:
Slow moving some, some anchor'd are,
Before Cavité rang'd along!

Threat'ning array!

                    Forts, batteries strong,
Support Spain's fleet from frowning shore,
Waiting their combin'd hail to pour
DEWEY's advancing ships among!

II.

The Flag-Ship seeks the foe straightway,
'Midst where the hostile cruisers lay,
Three battle-flags broad waving o'er!
Her eager consorts in her wake
Flaunt colors like some gala day,
Defying boldly sea and shore!—

Far the deep rumbles! Cruisers quake!
An earthquake shock! Wild billows shake
The Baltimore's near prow!
                    On high,
Like Hecla's seething geysers, fly
Torn waters foaming 'gainst the sky!

Again, nigh to the Raleigh's bow,
Huge deluge roars! From high falls loud,

Hurl'd from volcanic depths below—
Wild menace of a watery shroud!

III.

These huge mines, laid by wily Spain,
Sprang to destroy the ships in vain,
Whose prows unscath'd still cleave the main!

On, on! In battle's line array'd,
Majestic moved the sullen train:
Manila's guns, Cavité's bray'd,
Whose desp'rate missiles harmless stray'd,
Blending in combat's fierce refrain!

Mines hid below, mad shells above,
Exploding loud, as on they move,
While thund'ring forts, flame-belching ports
Wake, where the foe destruction courts!—

IV.

Reserve all fire!
    Signals proclaim
To men whose nerves vibrate with ire;
Who to retaliate desire;

Who to display high skill aspire,
To win the steadfast heroes' fame!

Ships, still as waiting earthquakes, breast
The waves—restrain'd the bolts of doom—
Their black breath rolling o'er each crest.
Commingling with dawn's lingering gloom:

Anticipant their gunners stand,
Impatient, anxious wait command;
While time the enemy improve,
Whose missiles shriek, crash round, above!—

The fighting-string in each man's heart
Sings, twanging taut, as when the dart
And quivering bow-string spring apart!

V.

On forward bridge, undaunted still,
Stands ADMIRAL, REECE, LAMBERTON;
Stands STICKNEY, with the *Herald's* quill:
Infinite skill guides CALKINS on,
Who stands unmoved the ship to "con;"

BRUMBY, Chief of the Signal Corps—
Ere long to raise that banner high
Above a new-gain'd realm to fly—
LIEUTENANT SCOTT, while combat blends
The scream of schrapnel, cannons' roar,
Look from the bridge:
      Unshielded stands
The Admiral, who here commands,
Each sense alert:
      Howling for prey,
Fierce battle's messenger of Death
Deep gores the deck, the bridge beneath,
Close where he stands!
      Above the group
A bursting shell, with fiery swoop,
Destroys the rigging close above,
Yet who shall shrink or feature move?

VI.

Head link in dread destruction's chain,
The Flag-Ship leads her dauntless train:
Save engine's throb and blower's whirr,

HOSTILE WATERS.

No sound yet emanates from her;
Nor yet may ready sponson smoke,
Nor yet has gun of DEWEY woke:

   Still as the pent-up hurricane,
Approaching steadfast as the storm,
When her black throats blaze deadly rain,
Monster of demon's fearful form!—
Death roaring from each blazing arm,
Shall the Olympia strike in vain?

THE BATTLE OF MANILA BAY, MAY 1, 1898.

Battle of Manila Bay.

I.

SPAIN'S hour has come! The dial of Time
At last ends her probation! Now
She falls, like Rome, 'mid seas of crime,
For slaughtered tribes; for many a vow
Unkept; for sages doom'd to bow
'Mid torturing flames: 'Neath axes' gleam
Heads roll'd when Thought faced every woe,
While bigot rage laid learning low:
To-day shall Freedom's powers redeem
From red crime's inundating stream!

* * * * * * *
* * * * * * *

II.

THE Maine remember! comes the word,
Which loud Olympia's spirits tell,
From boatswain's mate and gunners heard,
As close o'erhead a bursting shell
Hurls missiles with menacing yell!
Whose threat defies, to action stirs,
Till DEWEY now no more defers!

Five hundred throats take up the cry
From engine room to turret high!
On every ship, within, without
All join in that prophetic shout!
From men who wait, like coursers fret,
Who have not pulled a lanyard yet,
The sea-dogs' yelp flies toward the strand,
Whose vengeance now is close at hand!

III.

The Admiral makes prompt reply,
And toward the turret turns his eye:
"When ready, GRIDLEY, you may fire!"

And toward the enemy steams on,
As from its turret, wing'd with ire,
Roars the Olympia's forward gun!

"Fire as convenient!"
                    Ships astern
Signal'd from Flag-Ship's mast discern:
Baltimore, Boston joining in,
Their huge arms swell the battle's din!
   "Open all guns!"
                    At this command,
Bringing her port broadside to bear,
Olympia's craters shake the air!
O'er all, her turret's monsters blend
Their deep-toned diapasons grand!

Torn waters quake! Deep thunders roll!
While guns, from near Cavité's mole,
Where veers the foe, where tides are shoal,
With angry menace threat the goal!

Then, turning on her fiery way,
The dread Olympia seeks her prey,

Defied by blazing sea and shore,
Reina Cristina, Castilla:
Devoted twain!
    Projectiles gore
Their sides, which her fierce volleys pour,
While ships astern sustaining roar!

    IV.

 Then, Don Juan de Austria,
To board the adversary dread,
Advanced—all guns in fiercest play—
While broadsides strewed her deck with dead!
Till the Olympia's onslaught stern
Compelled her in retreat to turn;
By fires that quick and rapid play'd,
A veritable shambles made!

 And soon, in-shore, she sinking lay,
While DEWEY's squadron scour'd the bay!
Whose dauntless cruiser thenceforth led,
The circling line of battle's head,
Save when bold DWYER that honor had:

Gridley directs each deadly shower,
Rules this huge arsenal of power,
Fighting his ship from conning tower;
Manœuvering where war's tempests lower,
While denser falls the battle-cloud,
Enfolding like a giant's shroud!

V.

While fiery demons' shrieks appall
Halyards are shot from Brumby's hands,
Signaling, where the fore bridge stands,
The Admiral's commands to all:

A huge shell burst with fiery rain,
That Chaplain Frazier's view cut short!
Hurtling above the bomb-torn main,
'Mid flash, and roar, and loud report,
Gazing, with head thrust through a port;
Warn'd by this message to refrain,
This target for projectiles' sport
Was swift withdrawn, warn'd not in vain,
Ne'er to be so exposed again!

VI.

When SURGEON ABEL PRICE and aides,
With KINDELBERGER—whose high skill
Is not confin'd to surgic blades,
Handling as well the thinker's quill—
Arrang'd drugs, tourniquets that day,
To dress wounds in the forward "bay,"
'T was never dream'd no blood should spill,
No balm should pour, no scalpel score,
Save for hurt Spaniards on the shore!

As though charm'd lives these seamen bear,
Each cruiser of this deathless fleet—
Though missiles fell thick everywhere—
At roll-call mustered crews complete!

These gallant heroes Death defied,
Whose blood, in this most famous fight,
Flowed from few wounds, and those but slight,
While foemen, o'er a thousand, died
To sate the maw of Spanish pride
Before their flag sank out of sight!

VII.

War's horrors lightly smite the soul,
Enthused amid the strife, as here:
Swift as thought flies, at Death's quick call,
The World Beyond's strange scenes appear;
Surprise, allaying every fear
Of new existence: Spirits think;
Granting that all immortal are,
Who shall escape from thought, e'en there?
Instinctive, therefore, mortals shrink
O'er veil'd Eternity's mystic brink:

Powerless to repel the blow,
Expecting death, not knowing when
Or how this journey he must go,
'T were wisdom on the part of man
Nature's instructive page to scan,
Life's problem solve, work to the plan;
Illume the brain with Reason's ray,
Well freed from superstition's ban,
Let thought, untrammel'd, lead the way,
Spite what delusion's many say.

VIII.

Now, Raleigh, Boston, Baltimore
Upon the foe their batteries bore,
'Mong whom their raging missiles flew,
While Spain back answering volleys threw!

Thus, ships and forts hurl'd to and fro
Broadsides that blazed torn waters o'er;
And while fought each exhausted crew,
Dense-rolling smoke, of war's red hue,
Shut squadrons, forts and shore from view!

IX.

While CAPTAIN WILDES the conflict view'd.
Puffing cigar and using fan,
Where he, with aides, commanding stood,
Playing his part in battle's plan,
A mad shell o'er the Boston passed,
Near the Commander! Burst between!
Cut cleanly through the foremost mast—
Hurl'd lightning-bolts, war's sulph'rous rain!
The Captain nonchalant replied,

Though others winced who there stood fast,
Said, "We were lucky, gentlemen!"
Then, puffed at his cigar again:

X.

Helpful the man, inspir'd the thought—
Cooks' galleys' fires in fight subdued—
PAYMASTER MARTIN's coffee-pot
And spirit-lamp brown beverage brew'd,
Which he dispensed where gunners stood;
The fragrant berry's cheering sup,
Amid the battle, raging hot,
Keeping exhausted nature up,
Nor ceased till each received his cup:

A shell the ship's port-quarter found—
Burst!—filled with flame an Ensign's room!
Extinguished ere aught could consume;
Though DODRIDGE was not then at home,
Close at his post, by duty bound!

    *   *   *   *   *   *   *
    *   *   *   *   *   *   *

XI.

STEADFAST the gallant gunners stand,
Circling by blazing ships and strand,
Fast all the squadron's batteries play:

Then, ADMIRAL MONTOJO, rash,
Became the victor's hopeless prey:
Reina Cristina turned at bay,
Made toward the line her fatal dash!

Braving destruction, on she came
With bellowing guns!
                        A hell of flame!
Her crew devoted, undismay'd,
Vesuvius had as well invade!

She turned in flight, her mad course stay'd,
Her raid intrepid vainly made,
Or her crew's courage high display'd!

The fierce Olympia sent her shell,
Roaring the fleeing Spaniard's knell,
That struck astern, her hull sped through,
Burst 'midships! Her brave Captain slew,

BATTLE OF MANILA BAY.

Slaughter'd by scores her dauntless crew!
The Petrel's shot struck home as well—
Torn stem to stern, spared but the few!

XII.

She ventur'd, fail'd: Batter'd and torn,
Wounded to death, slow her return:
Nor shall the final stroke defer,
Dealt by the raging Baltimore!
The crew escaping flee to shore,
And red arms toward the Castilla—
Companion of her misery—
Reach o'er, beckoning for sympathy,
While one despair from both is born.

Spain's doom'd fleet drifts along the lee:
The Isla de Mindanio,
Don Antonio de Ulloa,
Villalobus and Rapido;
The Boston's prey, the Velasco;
Each craft destroyed, crushed small and great!
And now the crippled few but wait
Their sinking sisters' tragic fate:

XIII.

As when typhoons wild banners fling,
The battle's din rolls far away,
Echoing and re-echoing
From each side of that land-locked bay;
As War's throats multiplied their roar!
Dread sounds, such as, in earlier day,
Passed o'er subdued Corregidor
When Britain thundered at her door!

Then fell Manila! Then withdrew
The foe for ransom: though untrue
Iberia's pledge to Albion,
Still faithless, as in ages gone:
Whose conqueror never sought to sue
The beggar for the forfeit due.

HON. RUSSELL A. ALGER,
SECRETARY OF WAR.

Victory at Cavite.

I.

CAVITE sprawls the shore along
    Where yonder level sand-spit strays;
With arsenal, forts, batteries strong,
Low on the right, in the dim haze,
Where ships seek aid from many ways:
Here, ten leagues south Manila's seats,
Where the broad bay spreads beautiful,
O'er whose broad bosom soars the gull,
The duel rages of the fleets!

  Sultry the clime and hot the fight,
While flames on shore glow broader, higher,
The smitten walls one sea of fire,
While rolling vapors blind the sight!

Spain's Captains saw, defeated, dazed,
Their beaten ships—when vapors raised—
Though firing still, in fate's despite,
Crumbling piece-meal 'neath DEWEY's might!

 Doom'd ADMIRAL MONTOJO gazed
On ruin's field!
    Fleeing dismayed,
Ship after ship his flag displayed!
While each in turn in ruin blazed,
Annihilated, shattered, gored!
Remorseless guns, what shall evade?

II.

 A crippled cruiser from the foe
Fled toward Manila, firing slow:
Like NEMESIS awaked to wrath,
The Concord steamed along her path:

 "Sink or surrender!"
    High in air,
By the pursuer signal'd there,
Cut off escape, stay'd her career!

III.

Fifth time the foe's front thund'ring by—
As Spain's guns spoke less rapidly,
DEWEY about him cast his eye,
Said, as he scanned the conflict o'er:
"What time is it, LIEUTENANT REECE!"
"Seven-forty-five, Sir!" the reply:
"Breakfast-time! Signal, 'Fighting cease!'"
Then, that queer smile his features bore,
Peculiar to the Commodore:

'T was a strange, record-breaking fight!
A fleet in battle's midst withdrawn
That breakfast then might be brought on!
Forts, squadrons firing! Thrilling sight!
Where war-clouds dense obscure the sun!
Guns roaring! Missiles left and right!

IV.

Respite begun, the fleet, withdrawn,
Rode near the middle of the bay,
Northwest of where Cavité lay:

AT CAVITÉ.

The enemy still thunder'd on—
Destruction for the moment done—
And seem'd to surmise Spain had won,
Though inefficient every gun!

'Mid carnage wild, from Spanish arm,
Scarce man or ship had suffered harm
In all that rage of battle's storm!

Captains this interval repaired
To the Olympia to receive—
As signals hoisted high required—
Such orders as might be declar'd,
Relative to parts ships should play;
That now rode restful in the bay,
To end auspiciously the fray:

When orders were dispensed to all,
Congratulations on the day
Were tender'd by the Admiral,
Before his Captains went their way;
Ere each in his gig took his leave,
To worn and anxious crews relieve;

AT CAVITÉ.

Ere signals to the strife should call,
To give blows Spain might not retrieve!

V.

Since early morning's scant repast
All had endured protracted fast,
Which vigorous fighters ill could brook,
Their nerve-force drain'd:
      Enduring still,
Worn Nature claims her breathing spell:
Which, 't was assum'd, those signals meant,
The Admiral 'mid battle sent;
Though, doubtless, he could then have shown,
Most cogent reasons of his own:
State of his ord'nance should be known!

As hearty sustenance each took
The fragrant coffee, drink divine!
Sent new life through the weary line:

The enemy made sore complain,
In those reports which went to Spain,
That want of coffee was his bane!

Spoiling success; of strength made lack
To meet that early morn attack!
Proof the shrewd Admiral was right,
While Spain delayed to brew the cup,
To fight before the Don was up!

VII.

Wood strode the Petrel's deck again
'Mong resolute and eager men:
"We're going in the inside bay!"
Cheerily that staunch Captain said:
"One bold move more! Push on ahead!
And men, we're bound to win the day!
Don't waste a shot! Make each gun tell!
Seamen, you've done your duty well!"

These stirring words with wild joy fill'd
The hearts of all;
     Enthus'd and thrill'd.
The crews went wild—spontaneous yell'd!
When told, so far, no man was killed!

*   *   *   *   *   *   *

VIII.

SAID the Admiral: "Time to leave!
Everything all right, LAMBERTON?"
"Everything is, Sir, I believe."

The signal was to top-mast run:
"To quarters all! Get under way!"
And on the line moved to the fray!

When the tried fleet to battle drew
The Baltimore led on the line!—
With CAPTAIN DWYER's record fine,
His Chief declared 't was honor due,
Though her sides showed full many a scar,
Battered and bruised as veterans are—
O'er water-line a shell's track through,
Some seamen hurt, slight wounds and few!

IX.

The arms of Spain were faced again—
The conflict raged! Appalling view!
Guns bellowed to avenge the Maine,
By marksmen leveled tried and true!

Then, dauntless Dwyer's cruiser moved,
Whose broadsides wreck and ruin flung,
Slow-creeping steadily along
Close to the forts!
                    Spain's gunners proved
Impotent all to stay her course;
Or those embodiments of force
Behind her, belching shot and flame!
Whose men scored many a gallant deed,
Intrepid winning glory's mead,
The victor's crown, the hero's fame!

X.

Manœuvering, doubling to and fro,
Their thund'ring guns the foe assail,
Fast, furious flinging battle's hail;
The moving line one fiery glow,
While devastation marks their trail!

What patriot there is now aware
Such sentiment exists as fear?
As toward the enemy they go,

AT CAVITÉ.

Like doom relentless drawing near,
The war-cloud rent by cheer that greets
High rising o'er the roar of fleets!

XI.

While Evans with his motley flock
Wrought in the Olympia's hold, o'er head
They felt each missile's startling shock—
Withstood like Gibraltar's rock!
Yet, war's fierce turmoil failed to move
Those who munitions sent above,
Deep delving in the locker's bed,
For food the hungry guns that fed!

Stolid Mongolians wrought like men,
Displayed enduring spirit, then:
Through dust and heat and powder-stain,
Redeeming Yalu's conquered band,
When Japan's squadron swept their strand;
When all rejoiced o'er Freedom's gain,
To Dewey showed each toil-maimed hand,
And asked adoption by his land.

BRIG.-GEN'L HENRY C. CORBIN,
ADJUTANT-GENERAL.

Heroes of the Spanish-American War.

PART SIXTH.

The Surrender.

I.

MORE slowly Spain sends back reply:
    Forts silenced here, a battery there,
Explosions thund'ring everywhere!
Her ships in flaming ruin lie,
While rent walls yawn amid despair!

  To give the foe his final blow,
The Raleigh, Concord Boston, and
The Petrel signaled were to go,

Along the inner harbor's strand,
Engaging ships and forts inside,
Where Spain's foolhardy, stubborn will
Opposed chance to consummate skill;
And, though defeated, Fate defied,
While her brave men by hundreds fell!

II.

The missioned cruisers promptly file,
By ships and forts opposing sail;
While rapid gun, huge projectile,
Tell dread destruction's final tale!

The Petrel, naught from shoals to fear,
Would that wild bellowing shore assail
Alone!
      Light-draft, she dares to steer
Close to the cannons' mouths!
                Her hot
Volcanic storm of flaming rain,
At that range, with unerring shot,
Stills the last guns that speak for Spain!

Yon flag that red and yellow flies,
Spain's characteristics symbolize·
Her inhumanity, the red,
The hue of blood, of cruel dread;
Yellow, for avarice and gold,
That long crushed nations' histories told:

III.

The red and yellow fluttered down,
That here for centuries had flown,
O'er thousand isles its blight had thrown,
While Spain's lash made their peoples groan;
Where stern MAGELLAN was betrayed,
The first explorer to invade
These Eden islands of the Main,
And by their outraged chieftains slain.

Surrender's flags of white unfold
Where wreck and ruin's tale is told,
While up the Olympia's mast is run
The well-won legend:

        "Thanks, well done!"

IV.

After the glorious day was won,
To make capitulation good,
While war-clouds hung o'er fleet and town,
The Chief-of-Staff, with Captain Wood,
Was landed to negotiate,
Acquaint the vanquished with his fate:

They met the uncrushed, wily Don,
Who schemed, deferred, implored delay;
But found shrewd Captain Lamberton
In unprocrastinating way;
As both himself, with Captain Wood,
The treacherous Spaniard understood,
Who stood dazed, shocked at shrift so short!
This eminent diplomatic mind,
To the objector's wiles alert,
Had prompt surrender's details signed,
Sought the Flag-Ship and made report.

* * * * * * *
* * * * * * *

V.

The Petrel's Captain thanked his crew,
Whose deed, where thickest volleys rained,
Applause from all the fleet had gained;
Exhausted, joyous through and through,
All powder-burnt and battle-stained;
Whose woundless ranks high skill maintained;
Whose wearied groups contain not one,
Though deaf from detonating gun,
But sensed his Captain's gleeful tone:

"Well done, my lads, I'm proud of you!
And—Boatswain! Pipe all hands to 'splice
The main brace!'" Nautical, concise,
Well understood by seamen true!

VI.

Hilarious hour! Relaxed nerves rest;
Suspense is gone, reaction sprung;
Experiences, by all confest,
Tell how near pending dangers hung
While battle's thrilling music rung!

THE SURRENDER.

Thankful for life, limb, every soul
Grew reminiscent; veterans young,
Whose firm discipline reigned o'er all,
Now give good fellowship control.

 *   *   *   *   *   *   *
 *   *   *   *   *   *   *

VII.

BRAVE volunteers with SKIPPER HUGHES,
Of Petrel's men a half-a-score—
With whom ORDERLY KRAMER goes,
Whose graphic pen's description glows—
A ship's boat man:
     Each gleaming oar
Dips merrily the waters blue,
Nearing those ships Fates still pursue,
Cavité's smaller bay within,
Which by their guns had silenced been:

 The Skipper bids the work begin,
While hulks, shot-riddled, blend their glow,
And vanquished Spain makes loud complain!

THE SURRENDER.

From wreck to wreck with torch they row,
Complete their task, embark again,
While crackling sounds, and raging flames
Wrap barks that bear euphonious names:

Capture, destroy, the orders were;
Therefore, these wrecks, with ruin's glare,
Intensely heat the torrid air!

Flames from destruction's work refrain
While hulks afloat, though scarred, remain;
Ere long, 'neath wrecker's skilful hand,
With parts restored to cruise again,
'Neath Freedom's emblem guard the strand!

HON. CHARLES EMORY SMITH,
POSTMASTER-GENERAL.

After the Battle.

I.

THE Admiral on shore discerned
    The emblem of surrender; then
He said, as toward his staff he turned:
"I have as fine a lot of men
As ever yet on shipboard stepped,
With hearts strong as their ships equipped!"

  In presence of the whole command,
That 'round on the Olympia stood,
Cutting the Petrel's Captain short,
When handing in his ship's report,
DEWEY advanced with out-stretched hand,
Address'd the veteran:

AFTER THE BATTLE.

"Captain Wood,
I wish the English language could
Express the commendation due
To your grand self and gallant crew—
Your good ship's marvelous movements, too!

"'T will be my duty so to do,
America shall hear of you!
No words of mine are adequate,
Are beautiful and strong enough
To voice the commendation great,
Earned by men of such sterling stuff!
The truth what language can convey
Describing your grand work to-day?"

II.

The veteran said, whose years of cares
Revived in memories of the past:
"I've worked for those words fifty years
Through battle's roar and tempest's blast;
As my reward, they've come at last!
My crew, my ship, my pride my care—

We go where orders send us: There,
Wherever duty's path is clear—
Let fortune bring us foul or fair—
Where yon flag floats, its fate we share!"

* * * * * * *
* * * * * * *

III.

CAME the rejoicing Nation's thanks,
While all commissions were enhanced;
'Mong officers, marines, all ranks,
Worth well to higher lines advanced;
And, furth'ring commendation's plan,
Medals of merit decked each man;
While through each crew promotions ran,
The Baltimoreans sent a sword
As DWYER's richly earned reward!

DEWEY's sword! What magnificence!
Gold-handled, traced; blade damaskeened:
Inscriptions exalt elegance
'Mong rare and glittering gems entwined:

"To Admiral George Dewey: This
Gift of your grateful Country is."

Defender of her fame! To you,
Who won fair isles, broad treasure lands,
Congress elects this token due;
And honor's highest tribute sends
To him through whom the realm expands,
And whose fleet still her shores defends!

IV.

Now, from your Flag-Ship's mast-head high
No longer floats the old "burgee;"
Now, symbols on your flag that fly,
Waving, above the Asian sea,
"Admiral!" bid proud folds proclaim
Deservedly crowns a well-earned fame!

Skill'd diplomat! Here legislate
Till factions shall assimilate;
Your potent guns menacing bear,
Wise guardian of Manila!
Here,

AFTER THE BATTLE.

Your sway shall honor vindicate,
Shall arbitrate affairs of state,
Whose guardian care each race shall share,
Till friend and foe alike revere!

V.

Hold Aguinaldo's tribes in leash,
Till false advisors urge him on
To make with generous friends a breach,
Ensanguined stain their new life's dawn;
Mild AUGUSTINI's duty teach—
Spain's Viceroy, who his charge forsakes,
And with returning Teuton makes
Escape to Hong Kong, flees from care,
Passing the guard's averted eye,
Who bids safe journey courteously,
As the Augusta cruises by!

What though the Kaiser, grasping, proud,
Intrigues and schemes through bold designs,
His claims and airs are not allowed
While your guns guard the Philippines!

AFTER THE BATTLE.

VI.

Dewey ruled fair Manila Bay,
Held o'er all lawless factions sway;
Till on his Country's shores was fed
Obstruction, which rebellion bred!
Sent shells o'er arsenal and quay,
When Merritt's men in battle bled;
Where Otis fought, Greene, Anderson,
Brave Hawkins, Pennsylvania's son—
Till many a vict'ry Progress won;
Holds till Columbia's work is done,
Till insurrection's hosts have fled!

The Spanish Wolf has turned in flight
From bamboo bowers that joys invite;
Where Brumby raised that banner high,
Now kissed by Orient's golden smiles,
Whose stars and stripes through time shall fly,
Fair guardian of the Eden Isles.

MAJOR-GENERAL FITZHUGH LEE.

Spain's Lyre and Sword.

Argument.

Moorish Conquest of Spain—Addurrahman, the Omeyad prince—His capital, Cordova, "The Pearl of Andalusia"—Fall of Seville—The Cid Campæder—Spain's Heroic Age—Scenes in Moorish Grenada—Flight of Zobeide—Descent of the Spaniards from the Asturias—Boabdil—Scenes in the Alhambra—Eracilla, poet-soldier of fortune—His "Aurocania"—De Ruda, father of the Spanish drama—Lupe de Vega, the dramatic Cyclops—Cervantes: poet, soldier, lover—Heroic Age of Portugal—Camœns' life and times—Calderon—Modern Spanish poets—De Arcy's midnight vision—Decadence of modern Spain—Fancy's realm.

Spain's Lyre and Sword.

Romance of the Arab Conquest.

I.

'ER Calpé's Rock the Arab conquest broke,
   King RODERICK fell, Spain bent 'neath
      Islam's yoke;
Fair Andaluz with turbaned hosts ran rife,
Bold TARIC's hordes from Gaudaleté's strife:
Then sank the Goth, through JULIAN's treach-
      ery, low,
A father's vengeance for a daughter's woe.

Toledo, home of ancient Gothic kings,
Saw solemn ceremonial RODERICK crown
Ere wronged CLORINDA drew his ruin down;

Ere HERCULES unloosed his magic power,
When the rash king dared his forbidden tower.

II.

A ruined prince sought Andalusia's shores.
Fled to a throne, crowned by the kingless
    Moors—
The learned Omeyad, who subdued all foes,
Whose Capital in peerless grandeur rose;
His Cordova, where princes' sons were school'd,
Where Song's sweet voice and Beauty's man-
    dates ruled;
Yet, ABDURRAHMAN found no soothing balm,
And near his palace, in the evening's calm,
The monarch lorn mourned with his exiled
    palm:

Here the stern ruler bade fair Science reign,
Bade Song her highest excellence attain;
Damascene bards to realms fantastic soared,
Sustained in splendor by this Moslem lord;
Their warblings heard in halls of Far Cathay,

By ABU TEMAN, of the Tribe of Tay,
Live in the Moslem's precious scrolls to-day!
Live in the Arab's "Treasury of Song,"
Whose strains through Ind, o'er Afric roll along!

III.

Fair Seville 'rose, in fond delights secure,
A peerless pearl in Andalusia's core;
Whose famed Cathedral, rich in tracings grand,
Limned by MURILLO, great CAMPAGNA's hand,
Calls from Geralda's glittering statue high:
"What other joy with this bright scene can vie?

Here Castile's loveliness, 'neath Luna's ray.
Throngs fane, font, plaza decked in colors gay:
Enjoys bolero to mandolin's tongue,
Lists to romantic minstrel's ballad sung:

IV.

Old Guadalquiver, 'neath her olive groves,
Murmurs hard by of Beauty's jealous loves;

Where fiery rivals, her deep shades within,
'Mid spada's clash, wake fierce duello's din!
Whose bowers delicious lure to cool repose—
"Elysian Fields" Rome's conquering Cæsar
    chose;
For whose possession, mart, tower, garden,
    grove,
Rude Goth with Roman, Moor with Christian
    strove:
Wailed the Morisco when to Spaniard fell
The wealth, the beauty, grandeur of Seville!

V.

Oh, fondest theme of Spain's heroic lute!
Praising the CID her voice grows never mute—
Chivalric knight! Old Castile's warrior bold,
A nation's virtues in thy name are told!

Free-lance invincible! The Cross display'd
Till startling conquests jealous chiefs dismay'd;
Then, 'neath the Crescent—vengeance rules the
    hour!—
Leading the Moors through victory on to power:

Banished Alphonso's court—weep maid an
    dame!—
The Cid Valencia's Moslem king became!
Till—woeful day!—her portals 'gainst him
    close:
Again the Cid led Islam's Christian foes;
Raging in wrath, to crush the Panym's pride,
Valencia fell—ten thousand Moslems died!

VI.

What evil fortune to his banners passed,
When, broken-hearted, died the Cid at last!
Yet, stay—let not such generous knight decay!
Still shall he lead his followers to the fray,
Embalmed, in arms, secured on mailéd steed.
With couchant lance victory so oft decreed!

Rush clam'rous on the loud exultant foe!—
Lies not the Champion of the Christians low?
Behold! Advanced, a pale-faced horseman
    rides—
The dreadful warrior still his steed bestrides!

THE ARAB CONQUEST.

Tremble, ye Moors! Let cold fear smother glee!
'Mid panic, route and wild confusion flee!
Again the CID, on Andalusia's plains,
A final victory o'er the Moslem gains:

In fair San Pedro's Monastery grand,
Where Burgos' towers in lovely valleys stand,
By Chiefs surrounded, in his ivory chair,
Beside XEMENA, rests the CID from care;
While thousand lyres his virtues well maintain,
Still the chivalric pride of sunny Spain.

Love and War in Moorish Grenada.

I.

EIGHT centuries grand Moorish monarchs reign
In dazzling grandeur o'er heroic Spain;
From tower enchanted Magic's jeweled wand
Guides golden pageants o'er the dreamy land;
Weird strains melodious rise o'er fields of fate,
Exploits of Moor and Spaniard celebrate:

As monuments whose founders' names decay,
Speak of great deeds along Rome's Appian Way,
These rare old Iliads bear no line to tell
What minstrel sang so tersely, apt and well:

No artifice these vigorous lays employ,
Naught to embellish or the ear decoy;
The master painter's spirited portraits, dyed
In colors strong of old Castilian pride—
Majestic lineaments, stern, stately lays,
Whose melancholy sweetness ne'er decays:

II.

No pipe of peace, the war-horn's stirring strain
Mingles laments with requiums for the slain:
BERNARDO'S, CID'S, AGUILLAR'S trumpet blast
Comes from those far-off periods of the past;
Strife animates the brave hidalgo's breast,
Whose battle-axe whirls o'er the Moslem crest!
Whose spears achieve, whose challenge-trumpets ring!
Whose deeds of daring mail-clad minstrels sing.

Fade from the view these Gothic spirits stern,
Whose sinewy forms with dauntless valor burn;
A world more dazzling rises on the view
Of gorgeous pageants, dyes of brilliant hue!

III.

Grenada's plazas with exotics glow,
Through greenest banks Xenil and Darrow flow.
Where Andaluzia's golden sun-light falls
On fluttering scarfs, o'er tents and palace walls:
  Ho, for the bull-fight! Speeds the fair array!
Heralds proclaim XARAFA's wedding day!
Gay Moorish knights, with steeds as white as milk,
Array'd in gambesons of crimson silk,
With scarf of blue and crimson talahie,
Through Vivarambla's square like whirlwind fly!

  Each knight hurls high his keen Damsascus blade,
Whose ancient maker ne'er his art betrayed;
Nor can to-day such temper'd steel be made,
Though thousand smiths, with subtlest skill, essayed
The damaskeening of the metal bright;
Whose inwrought tracings blaze in golden light,

And myriad colors, interlacing blend,
In sunlight glancing as it meets the hand
Adroit that grasps the quick-returning steel,
Whose watering shades the fountain's hues re-
    veal:

IV.

Brilliant imagination rules his mind,
Quick to conceive, to subtlest wit inclin'd;
Sagacious, varying like the desert wind;
Lithe-form'd, acute, hospitable to a fault,
Dies for the guest who shares his bread and
    salt!

His warrior soul, by poesie's graces charm'd,
Serves destiny, by eloquence quick warm'd;
Avenges wrong with never-flagging zeal,
Biding his time with Fate's relentless steel!

Thus to the tournament they gaily ride;
From gilded balconies on either side
Dark Moorish beauties lean to view the sight,
Whose bright eyes gleam from many a lattice
    light:

V.

The lists are up, armed champions appear!
Loud din of cymbals blends with ringing cheer!
Steeds prance, rear, wheel! Reeds shiver with
    the charge!
Battered and torn see many a knight emerge!
ALBOIN's arm each challenger o'erthrows,
On whom the turbaned king the bride bestows;
Whose gem-lit beauty glows like starry night,
Ending a day of feasting, love, delight.

* * * * * * *
* * * * * * *

VI.

GRENADA sleeps, her day of turmoil flown,
While nightly specters stalk beneath the moon:
Soft Xenil glows; dark Darrow's water's flow
Round red Alhambra's terrace deep below;
In whose tall towers a Christian captive lay,
Till friends, for ransom, bore the youth away:
Sweet Zobeide admired his lofty mien,
And learned to love e'er mountains rose be-
    tween:

LOVE AND WAR.

A Christian lover! Evil must befall!
Vail, lovely princess, from thy castle wall—
Hark! Softest sounds the warm winds waft within—
'T is his dear voice, his warning mandolin—
"Haste, haste thee, Love! Thy ladder light unfold,
Formed of thy turban with belt gemmed in gold!
Thy palfry waits concealed in yonder shade,
Champing to bear his mistress, trembling maid!

"Mount, ZOBEIDE! With me seek Xenil's shore,
To breast its wave and fear no parting more!"
Love checks each sigh, beguiles the clinging lass,
Speeding beyond dun Alpuxarras' Pass!

* * * * * * *
* * * * * *

HARK! 'Tis the silver clarion's warning sound!
Loud rolls the Moorish attabal around!

Sweeping down from Nevada's snowy pass,
Across the Vega, crimsoning its grass,
Asturia's hordes, sons of the Goth, appear!
Daughters of Islam, wail with pallid fear!
"Woe, woe is me, Alhama!" chants the seer!
The Christians to Grenada's gate draw near!
From high Alhambra's towers the cross is flung,
Mid valorous deeds by Moor and Spaniard sung.

VII.

Grenada, ages, gives her greenest bays
To Earth's wise sons; in Honor's seat arrays,
Till Moorish power with doom'd BOABDIL falls,
When desecration seeks Alhambra's halls;
And Afric's shores send back the exile's sigh,
Whose desolate lords in her vast deserts die!

'Neath dominating Mountains of the Sun,
Her red towers draped in somber shadows dun,
Glooms the Alhambra o'er her Vega plain,
Where Moorish Chieftains led their regal train;
Grand as the Greek Acropolis she sits,
While woe's drear garb her desolation fits—

Mourning amid her gardens desolate,
Like slighted Beauty for her lost estate:

The blooming paradise before her yields
Myriads of fruits, where smile a thousand fields;
Citron and vine shade rich hidalgo's seats;
Through grove and bower gleam ancient kings'
　　　　retreats.
Whence oft BOABDIL led his turbaned band
To check the steel-clad hosts of FERDINAND;
Or climbed COMARES' tower to view the strife,
While o'er his realm raged red destruction rife!

VIII.

Child of Romance, Alhambra's arches range,
Ponder and dream, muse sadly o'er the change;
Frowning in gloom, perched on her terrace
　　　　height,
Those walls were once the home of fond delight!

Arabia, Syria, Turkey, Ind. employ
Their rarest arts to grace this realm of joy;
Whose fountains fall in marble as of yore,

Murmur and sob for glories now no more;
Whose marvelous tracings—modern art's despair—
With trailing Arabasques, mosaics rare,
Translucent fillet, radiating leaf,
Gauzy and light, stone-lace in frail relief,
E'en tinted Koran texts skilled YUSEF planned,
Stay the long centuries' remorseless hand!

From these light galleries beheld below
Matron and maid bright pageants ebb and flow;
Veil'd to dark eye, to Koran precepts true—
Though what could hide such loveliness from view!
Those luring smiles, those stolen glances dear,
Those tokens thrown to favored cavalier!

IX.

Sweet LYNDARAXI, thou wert wont to gaze
Where thy rose-garden 'neath this casement lays;
And thou hast with the harem's beauties flown,
And for thy soft lute night-winds sadly moan.

What gay throngs gathered at the Myrtle
    Pond!
The Lions' Court with arches high beyond!
Most charming chamber of the Sisters Two,
What loveliness was hidden here from view!

    In these boudoirs, dreaming on divans round,
Blazing in gems, princesses heard the sound
Of lute and song: Damascene poets, claimed
For princes' consorts, gave recitals famed,
Where came the learn'd from every splendid
    court,
Where dancers, soothsayers' arts relieved light
    sport:
Embodied dream, pageant too fair to last—
Bagdad, Damascus rise from out the past!

Spain's Poet Heroes.

I.

THROUGH Song's charmed land, wand'ring 'mid legend's shade,
Where storm, rout, conquest all the scene pervade,
From hist'ry's dawn, follow the length'ning years
Till stronger light in CHARLES' day appears—
When intellect strove through rapine, blood and tears—
When Castile hails her Poesie's Golden Age!
Scans GARALASO'S ALMOGRAVER'S page,
Who from Italia's smooth and lucid tongue,
Conveys the charm that play's their verse along.

II.

Gallant ERCILLA, fields of conquest view
Beyond strange seas where dangers dire pursue!
True fortune's soldier, lured beyond the Main
'Mong Peru's tribes, Auraco's savage plain;
The Realms of Gold, where fierce PIZARRO's chain
Limbs unaccustomed binds with cruel pain:

Here the dread conqueror rends the gem-lit crown
From Inca ATHAHUALPA's forehead brown!
And here the blended blood of Castile reigns,
Full warmly glows in dusky damsels' veins;
Affection's dark-eyed Children of the Sun,
Through all whose years time's sad romances run.

Heroic bard, thy glowing line record
On leathern trappings, scraps the camps afford;
Where comrades round weary and wounded lie,
Fierce captive caiques roll the glistening eye;

'Mid clashing arms, where gath'ring swarms appear;
Where poison'd arrows whizz! shrieks wound the ear!
Mark, while they strike, thy countrymen's bold deeds,
Till night-gloom falls, and war's turmoil recedes:
What graphic colors limn the Indian's life,
His home, his loves, wild valor in the strife!
Till Aurocania's stirring scenes appear,
Pictures from life, the war-drum, helm and spear.

III.

Ercilla, thou didst countless dangers know!
Stretched not thy neck the murd'rous axe below?
Fierce rival's spada now thy life demands,
Exiled from Spain, roaming in hostile lands;
Attending Philip to Queen Mary's throne,
Where Britain's fétes the ill-starred nuptials crown—

Obscurely dying, all thy worth forgot,
'Mid want and woe, the poet's thankless lot!

IV.

Four bards immortal light Spain's drama's dawn:
RUDA, CERVANTES, VEGA, CALDERON;
While Albion sees her chiefest names appear,
And, o'er the Pyrenees, Gaul starves MOLIERE!
Five marvelous decades! Britain, France, Castile
The greatest geniuses of time reveal!

V.

Long glad Spain laughed o'er RUDA's mimic show,
Whose genius taught her Humor's garb to know;
Who saw with joy gay Comedy's Prince arise,
First to portray life's myriad vagaries:

Oh, could the Muse DE RUDA's play-house paint,
His sceneless walls, his motley hearers quaint;

Where through no trap-doors pallid ghosts arise,
No angels fall from heaven through painted
 skies;
In combat fierce Christian nor Moor appears,
Nor mandolin the ballad-singer bears;
Yet, here the boy CERVANTES learned his art,
In burlesque garb rare wisdom to impart,
Secured the charm that rules the human heart:

From camp to town the genial RUDA stray'd,
Kissing his hand to every chambermaid;
The people's joy, Don, peasant loved his name,
Whose well-mark'd types from walks familiar
 came;
Who gave the stage clown, harlequin, buffoon
To serve great masters in the drama's noon.

VI.

Behold great LOPE DE VEGA passing near,
While Madrid's streets echo with cheer on cheer!
Exhaustless mine, the "Rhyming Potosi!"
"Phœnix of Spain!" strong Nature's prodigy,

Whose powers of thought, colossal breadth of
    mind,
Creative speed, leave all the world behind!

  A truant boy whose large eyes round and
    clear
To teachers say, high genius bideth here!
Each day, long years, mind's vast creations
    hurl'd
Plays, epics, lyrics countless on the world!
What life of man so crowded full of fame,
What luster lights the mighty poet's name!
Spain's synonym for loveable and fair,
Whose presence rings her joy-bells everywhere!
Whose life's anomalies countless fountains
    drain—
Dramatic Cyclops of the iron brain,
Shall Nature LOPE DE VEGA frame again?

  Armada's soldier, duelist, lover, priest,
Inquisitor, with power and honors graced;
Whose flagellations crimson cloister walls,
Fasting till weak, exhausted nature falls;

Till Death's draped chamber echoes with his
    cries,
Of man's neglect complaining, weakly dies!

VII.

    In that same street, rebuking Vega's sighs,
In patient poverty Cervantes lies;
Expiring while his features frame a smile—
E'en perishing, would grizzly death beguile!
Life's quenchless humor present to the end,
Foretells his hour to one unchanging friend:

    Spain's genial favorite, destined to explore
New regions quaint on human life's wide shore!
Transcendent genius Hoyos soon discerns
Bright in his pupil's boyish bosom burns:
Loving the Muses from those earliest years,
What varying fortune turbulent appears,
Though brief those joys life like to his endears.
While yet his country Europe's councils led,
Ere Freedom, Thought, her Chivalry were dead,
Ere axe and flame her sons of Science fed.

VIII.

At Rome, the Cardinal's scribe, thirsting for fame;
Fighting the Turk, lured by Colona's name—
When Moslem galleys ride Lepanto's bay,
When Christian arms meet Moslem's proud array;
When Venice, Spain and Pope their fleets combine,
And Egypt's ships with Turk's and Arab's shine—
Though burning fevers rage in every vein,
Seek ye CERVANTES where death's missiles rain!
Where Alexandria's princely standards play,
Boards her king's barge, bears Egypt's flag away!

Through victory's shout the hero calls his band:
Alas, the maim'd right arm, the sunder'd hand!
Sad mutilation, view'd with soldier's pride—
Dread loss, Spain's thankless PHILIP ill supplied;

When life grows drear where is thy valor's
   mead,
Who bled to glut that cruel monarch's greed?

IX.

On hard-fought fields, by Navarino's walls,
Where Sovereign's will or patriot duty calls,
Behold CERVANTES' plume in thickest fray.
Till home, love, country call their friend away:

Scarce danced his galleon o'er the waters
   green—
Homeward! Pirates!—The Algerine!
In vain the hand-full charge the swarming host,
The shackl'd captives tread the Paynim's coast:

Five weary years the slave of ANAOUT.
Bound, bastinadoéd, scourged by cruel knout;
Recapture, torture, follows desp'rate flight—
Till ransomed, Spain, friends bless the poet's
   sight;
Where laurels wait, a noble lady's love.
Till want at last o'er worth shall victor prove.

Immortal author of QUIXOTE's page,
Reformer, satirist of a frivolous age!
"Child of Disturbance," named La Mancha's tale,
Conceived, planned, wrought in dismal Turkish jail;
Where hopeless captives pace their dreary round,
Where tortures, groans and clanking fetters sound:
What sword shall maim, what hold thy tireless mind,
What cankering chain imagination bind?

Midst rest and ease the child of Fancy grows,
Where murmuring springs invite to cool repose;
The barren Muse impregnates with delight,
Swift admiration following her flight:
CERVANTES' genius seeks his native shore,
Beyond the gloom behind his dungeon door;
Whose name, o'er all her bards, let Spain revere,
In every clime, to every people dear.

Decline of Spain's Golden Age.

I.

RISE CALDERON, bard of romance, to soar
  In pious pomp, through realms un-
    found before!
Thy Muse prolific grapples giant Thought,
Magnificent, in burnish'd grandeur wrought:
What joyous pæans through thy pages lurk!
Exalted themes, "Creation's" wond'rous work!
Grand poet, let exalted anthems ring,
Oppress'd with honors from thy doting king!

Most fêted courtier, by Spain's monarch sent
'Mid the Low-Country's wars: A decade spent,
Till PHILIP's summons bids thee celebrate,
Deck Austria's Princess' splendid bridal fête:

DECADENCE.

Favorite, thy verse elaborate care displays,
'Mid sumptuous splendor's ever-dazzling blaze!
Last of the race Romance's summit roam'd,
From flower to star sang Nature's world endom'd.

II.

Spain's Golden Age with these grand names appears,
Declines with these, sinks through degen'rate years:
A deepening twilight o'er the period falls,
Through which the wand'ring minstrel faintly calls;
Where Poesie's shrunk streamlet fitful flows,
Twining 'mong rivers vast of rhyméd prose;
Though bards there be, like beacons by the way
Who light the gloom with song-land's rythmic ray,
Till deepening gloom hides Spain's heroic day.

* * * * * * *
* * * * * * *

DECADENCE.

III.

FIERCE LUCITANIA made her thinkers groan,
As did Jerusalem her prophets stone:
Starvation, wheel, Inquisitorial flames,
Rack, dungeon, exile long quenched lustrous names;
Beneath each bigot censor's fierce control,
She chained benignant Progress, warped the soul!
Like her mad sister, strew'd Iberia's plain
With mangled forms of bards and sages slain,
Men of high purpose, great in thought's domain!

E'en here, like beacon lights, great kings would rise,
Whose rule enlighten'd lit Time's gloomy skies
ALPHONSO Fourth, grand PEDRO First appears,
While roll around the sad, romantic years;
Benignant rulers, men of mighty minds,
At whose high courts learning warm welcome finds,
Whose intellect clear no superstition binds.

IV.

Proud Portugal's exalted age behold—
Great poets, warriors, navigators bold!
Though Afric's storms wreck, India's sun defies,
Chivalrous courage, fiery enterprise
Urge daring spirits to their scorching clime,
Whose songs with wars, wrecks, ocean-surges
    chime:
From home, love, ease, to separation doom'd,
Sad melancholy's tone their lyres assumed;
Contrasting strange with action's restless fire,
That bids men rove and, seeking fame, expire!

Bold spirits of the Levant, venturous, strong,
Congenial soul sings your sublimest song!
Discoverers grand of India's torrid shore,
Whose gold and jewels in your coffers pour,
Who 'round dread Good Hope's gloomy cape
    first ranged,
And course of commerce of the world so chang'd;
Who many a shore made Lucitania's prize—
Let CAMOENS with your own great names arise!

V.

Bard of his country's romance, unsubdued,
He dared all climes, courting vicissitude;
Exiled from all his steadfast spirit loved,
'Mid war's fatigues, strange scenes his spirit moved!
Grief scourged his youth, nor ceased till death's sad close
Completed life's long Iliad of woes!

Unhappy lot! striving 'gainst Islam's host,
Banished by calumny to India's coast;
Cheered by good fortune in Macao's clime,
Building the Luciad, crowning work sublime!
In that lone grot above the sounding sea,
Found mighty inspirations, boundless, free!
Fame's cavern wild, to curious travelers shown,
With CAMOEN's named, through lengthening ages known!

VI.

Here mused; here celebrated souls renowned
Who sailed strange seas, dared savage shades profound;

Where frown'd the dark-browed Spirit of the Cape
Whose thund'rous wrath what seaman may escape!
Heard Good Hope's surges sound DE GAMA's doom,
Whose venturous barque the waters wild entomb;
Bade men's hearts bleed o'er fair DE CASTRO's woes,
Whose bosom crimsoned swords of jealous foes:
Torn from her babes, pressed to her tear-dewed face,
Because her blood flowed from a hated race!
Soared with light Fancy in her boldest flight,
Where graceful nymphs in bower and stream delight;
Where Joy's fair isle floats in the emerald sea,
Home of fond love, bright Beauty's progeny.

VII.

In stormy Macon's mouth, by Goa's coast,
His homeward barque in wildest breakers lost,

Engulfed by seas, his strong arm smites the wave,
Its fellow bears the Luciad high to save—
His dearest treasure—from a threat'ning grave!
Faint not, strive on! Held in that conquering clasp
That peerless epic which the æons grasp!
Most priceless gem in Lucitania's crown,
To days degen'rate telling past renown;
Wide o'er the land gathering a deathless fame,
King, courtier, peasant lauding CAMOENS' name!

Though jealous foes hurl persecution's dart,
Steadfast to right, still uncorrupt of heart:
Truth clears his name: Escaped from prison-bars,
Again contending 'mid the Lucian wars,
Pierced through the eye, one window to the soul
Remains to light life's pathway to its goal:
Oh, mightiest grief that darkening life to cross,
Called to lament lovely ATTAYDA's loss!

VIII.

Broken by hardship, scorch'd by India's sun.
Life's course well nigh through toils and dangers done,
One friend, the slave, ANTONIO yet remains
To beg the bread the flagging life sustains
Till—in the lazar-house—dead in his rags.
A winding-sheet the good Priest JOSEPH begs!

By CAMOENS' bed-side, in the sombre gloom,
The kind friar writes thus in the Luciad's tome:
How miserable a thing!   What fortune hard,
So great a genius perishing without reward!
Sailing the seas through countless leagues of storms;
Through India's fevers bears his country's arms;
Maimed, exiled, weary, studying night and day.
Toil without profit wearing life away;
Like as the spider spins his web for flies,
A fruitless fame, the unsubstantial prize.

* * * * * * *
* * * * * * *

IX.

Spain's later patriot-poets, jealous, blind,
Throughout their verse tradition's strains entwined;
Whose lines unpolished in abundance flow.
Nor philosophic doubt, self-question know;
Love, Nature, legend find untrammeled place,
With metric histories of their fading race—

All save De Arcy's verse, whose blameless hand
And voice prophetic warns his native land:
"Onward!" his cry; "Spain, be alive to-day!"
Irrevocably dead, the past shall know decay;
Old systems, faiths, punctilious laws enthrall,
Progression's voice sends forth inspiring call.
The modern spirit all his song pervades,
Unsatisfied, aspiring, lights and shades:

X.

Placed early 'mid politic fields of strife,
The earnest, serious purpose of his life
Soon fixed him foremost in his country's eye—

Gave Valadolid's son her honors high:
Governor at Barcelona, Madrid's sage,
The statesman bard does honor to his age!

Around, the Carlists' futile conflict raged.
His prescient page their sure defeat presaged—
Hail, "Cries of Combat!" most distinctive lays:
Royal Academy, confer your bays!
From friendless indigence his sterling worth
Has placed the poet with the great of earth:

XI.

De Arcy thus portrays, in vision grand,
His solemn warning to his native land:
In the great Philip's monastery gray,
Where mould'ring monarchs sleep in cold array.
In ghostly garments wrapped, in midnight
    gloom,
Its royal founder rises from his tomb!

Toward the grand organ, gorgeous rear'd in
    pride,
The frowning phantom bends its stately stride;

The skeleton hand along the gamut flies—
Above the key-board blaze the hollow eyes!
Hark, the Miserere's solemn strains arise!
Whose tones deep-rolling through drear vaults resound,
Rousing Spain's ancient kings from sleep profound!

Their grim procession by the poet moves.
Whose race degen'rate each stern shade reproves—
Far roll weird echoes through dark isles away,
The lordly phantoms vanishing in decay:
The mighty Philip rears his bony hand,
With shrunken finger marks the fading band;
Queries Death's hollow voice: "Shall these end all?"
Then sinks to dust beneath his mould'ring pall!

XII.

In hopeful strain soars Arcy's "Hymn of Peace,"
Where joyous pæans presage Spain's release:

Bard of his country's saddest grieving hours,
His lyre exults when fall her blighting powers;
Whose Muse enlightened problems deep engage,
With all the great upheavals of the age;
Unshrinking, bold, truth stamps each pregnant
    thought,
While melancholy views the ruin wrought.

   *   *   *   *   *   *   *
   *   *   *   *   *   *   *

FAIR FANCY! Spirit of immortal dreams,
Whose children people mountains, forests,
    streams;
Whose pinions, poised o'er Joy's exalted height,
Pierce the glad regions of supreme delight;
Riding PUCK's girdle with the lightning's wing
Where rainbows bend; gives zest to everything;
Inspiring spirit of the fair and grand,
Your glow adorns all forms of sea, air, land!

Most immaterial of immortal things,
Impalpable as perfume's viewless wings,
Art's kind purveyor since Time's march begun,

Whence genius lives whose bright dome wooes
 the sun!
 here ambient suns whirl flaming through the
 skies.
Far, fast and free in flight untrammeled rise,
While your far flight all time and space defies!

 Boundless, undying Fancy, is your home—
'Tis FairyLand; dim, shadowy realms of gloom;
The coral caverns of the sounding Main;
'Midst forest depths; on flowery prairie plain;
Where Cashmere's gardens give sweet odors
 birth—
In fiery bowels of the molten Earth!

 Guide of the weary in their search for rest.
By beatific visions kindly blest,
You lift life's grievous burden from the mind.
Hope's realm revealing like a Fairy kind;
Your radiant charm brings toil-bound thought
 release,
Whose soul-exalting visions picture peace:

DECADENCE.

When shapes Cyclopean shake the fierv shore,
When Neptune's realm far quakes beneath the roar,
Why seeks fair Fancy War's ensanguined field?
For such fair guest shall Ruin tribute yield?
Why comes bright Fancy from glad realms of rest,
Where life's red current stains the warrior's breast?
'Tis to proclaim that when strife's clouds shall clear,
New forms of thought harmonious shall appear!
Evolving Nature stamps upon her page
Types of crude forms that marked each earlier age;
Reformed through conflicts, elemental rage;
Like the wild storm that purifies the skies,
Whose lightning burns death's poisons as it flies,
Each vicious force obstructing Progress dies.

HEROES OF SANTIAGO.

AN EPIC POEM.

BY THEODORE F. PRICE.

Uniform with the present volume, the above stirring heroic poem, which is now passing through the press, will soon be issued; comprising nearly three hundred pages, in elegant style of print and binding, profusely illustrated with portraits of military and naval leaders, war views, etc., completing the story, with the poetry and romance of the war.

This is designed to be a companion volume to "Heroes of the Spanish-American war," and, like its predecessor, is specially adapted as a gift-book, and token of remembrance of the officers and men of the Army and Navy.

This realistic poem takes up the theme of the war where the present volume leaves off; dealing with Shafter's operations about Santiago, from the embarkation at Tampa till the surrender of Toral, with much that followed, including the taking of Porto Rico by General Miles.

This work will contain thrilling and graphic accounts of the daring deeds of the Rough Riders under their dashing leaders Roosevelt and Wood; a stirring and vivid description of the sinking of Admiral Cervera's fleet by Sampson's squadron under Schley; together with the chief episodes connected with the more prominent transactions; told in smooth, melodious verse, much of which is well adapted to the purposes of recitation.

The "Heroes of Santiago" embraces, along with the above, a series of vividly drawn poetical character-sketches, pen-pictures and descriptions of deeds of individual heroism; also of the sublime and beautiful scenery that formed the environment, the picturesque isles and waters of the Gulf.

Either volume or both: "Heroes of the Spanish-American War," and "Heroes of Santiago," the two forming one complete whole: Price, by mail, $1.25, each. Address:

THEODORE F. PRICE,
Cape May, New Jersey.

www.ingramcontent.com/pod-product-compliance
Lightning Source LLC
Chambersburg PA
CBHW021406230426
43666CB00006B/654